"THE PRESIDENT"

STANLEY WATSON

THE GIFT OF LOVE
*
THE FRUIT OF LIFE

"THE EPPIEOLOGIST"

by Epaphroditus "Eppie" Elkahan

iUniverse, Inc.
New York   Bloomington

THE PRESIDENT

The Eppieologist

Copyright © 2009 by Epaphroditus "Eppie" Elkahan

iUniverse books may be ordered through booksellers or by contacting:

iUniverse
1663 Liberty Drive
Bloomington, IN 47403
www.iuniverse.com
1-800-Authors (1-800-288-4677)

ISBN: 978-1-4401-5636-6 (pbk)
ISBN: 978-1-4401-5635-9 (cloth)
ISBN: 978-1-4401-5637-3 (ebk)

Printed in the United States of America

iUniverse rev. date: 11/19/2009

ACKNOWLEDGEMENT

From the center of my HEART

When I was created centuries ago I was the happiest human on the planet, world, and universe, until my Ego, Passion, Ambition, Narcissism, and Neurosis created a plethora of events that induced excruciating pain and agony for my family and friends. During that negative environment two of my reasons for living were removed from the physical and emotional sections of my heart and world, Anselm Duchaussee (1993), and Adrienne Duchaussee (1996).

As an expression of my deep and devastating pain, anger and hatred my choices were hate and die or love and live.

Life was chosen by my Eppieologist, so I decided to live and love again and during my reconstruction and reconnection my creative passion and energy reached its pinnacle.

"The President" was created and Copy Written in 1997 from the chemistry of all my love, joy, pleasure, and pain. YES I DID! "The best is yet to come, the sun will shine again."

With all my love, passion and respect I dedicate this book to my five children: Anselm, Adrienne, Anjurle, Arveanka, and Areon. To my three grandchildren: Anselm III, Jazea, and Nasir. To my Parents: Cecil Richard and Auldith Duchaussee. To my sister and brothers: Dolores, Neville, Anthony, and Michael. To my family's strength and support: Kathy-Ann, Karen, Lisa, Micheal, Kwasi, Krista, Stefen, Jase, Chenelle, Athea, Percy, Arlene, Dorren, Delevan, Ketura, Melody and Beverley. And to: Falisha Lafay.

My open-ended praise and respect to these creative high end writers, for their time, love, support, collaboration, consultation and partnership: C. Richard Winn, Skip Press, Joy Darlington, Iris Bowlay, and Tri Qui Di.

And to my Italian Angel and Muse, Esther Chighine of Como; opposites do not attract they complement, inspire, motivate and stimulate the passion and determination of it's benefactor. You have contributed an invaluable and price less treasure that keep the spark that lights the flame of love in me, so I can share it with the world. Ti Amo!

To every human that I ever meet weather positive or negative influence, friend or foe, you contributed to making me who I am today, thank you, may you find your reason and purpose for being created, let your sun shine so that your energy will help you to reach the stars.

If you have stored up Anger and Pain that you cannot put in it's proper place use the smooth, warm and relaxing gift of love to help you re-visit the origins of your hurt and pain, so you can connect and redirect the flow of love to your heart. Only by loving again will you live again.

It's all Eppieological from my Eppieology and from your Eppieologist.

Epaphroditus "Eppie" Elkahan

Live, Love and Die with Passion!!!!

Foreword

I believe when I was born I sought for an answer not knowing the question: "Why was I born? Why am I here?" So, my journey began as a child looking to unlock the dreams of my heart in search of a treasure that I could give to the world. Bound within my own flesh, I heard the cries of the people and saw the brokenness of empty promises. I knew even within my struggles, my pain, and through my losses there was a treasure within; for I saw chains upon the hearts of men, women and children and I said: "Cry Freedom! For light has dawned." My inspiration of hope has shined forth like a star in the night, and the question has been answered. I was born to be an inspiration to the people of the world and that is how "The President" came to life. It's a story about a boy who found hope, a man who dreamed and journeyed until he found a "key" that will unlock the heart. May this key of love, inspire, strengthen, and free you.

Live, Love, and Die with Passion.

Cry Freedom!

Prologue

"THE PRESIDENT"

THE GIFT OF LOVE
*
THE FRUIT OF LIFE

"THE EPPIEOLOGIST"

The United States first African American president, Stan Watson, possesses a unique and special power. Although it may be assumed that his primary support comes from the African American community, this is actually more a stereotype than reality.

Stan Watson is loved by the majority of Americans but also by leaders and citizens throughout the world. And in a world where separatism and racism have become epidemic, Stan, by crossing political, social, religious, and business boundaries, has penetrated the public psyche with a different kind of passion.

Stan's intellect is bare-boned, raw, and gutsy. Armed with a unique educational mix from Harvard, the Military, and the Internet, Stan is also savvy at doing backdoor deals and engages, when necessary, in the corporate manipulation and political maneuvering that have been the lifeblood for most successful politicians.

Unlike most politicians, however, Stan is a mastermind at the game of strategy. His fluency in six different languages (Japanese, Chinese, Russian, German, French, and Arabic) makes him colorless to most. He does not typify the stereotype of the American black. He has reached the pinnacle of success, achieving what many would have believed to be impossible—the presidency. Yes, there are naysayers and those who would rather see him dead, but the frontline and behind-the-scenes support that he has garnered (through both transparent and covert means) have positioned him as a representative not only of people of color but of whites who have "forgiven" him for being black.

President Watson has, in essence, injected his spirit and passion into the world's emotional playground. With great precision and wisdom, he massages the fundamental needs and desires of humankind. With every stroke of his hand, with every nuance in his smile, with every utterance of his word, President Watson touches the world. To many, this is too much power for a black man, but for most, the challenge and the risk is worth it.

"THE PRESIDENT"

"THE EPPIEOLOGIST"

Treatment

By

Epaphroditus "Eppie" Elkahan

A group of African Americans—ALEX STUART RUTHERFORD, Department Chair, WILSON RUSTIN POWERS, FRANKLIN JUNIUS STEADMAN, and FLOYD KVAMME DAVIDSON, members of Sigma Pi Phi, code name, "HUMPTY DUMPTY"—secretly meets at Harvard University to discuss "the Twenty-first Century Plan," a project they've been working on for fifty years. They sit at a conference table, each looking through papers, as EDNA SESSIONS ADDINGTON, a.k.a. "EDY," an African American beauty, walks around the table. The Twenty-first Century Plan is a blueprint for the enrichment and elevation of the massive African American underclass. This plan will provide the educational, economical, social, political, and ethical foundation to prepare America for the twenty-first century. After the plan is reviewed and accepted unanimously, it is ready to be executed, but there is one problem: where would the money to finance the project be found?

High in the Swiss Alps, it is 5:00 AM in the dead of winter. We see a high alpine road that dead-ends at an armored entrance door on the side of Mt. Dufourspitze. A high-tech, high-concept Volvo snowmobile is parked against a stone fence nearby. Above the door, a surveillance TV camera swivels back and forth, surveying the area.

Above the mountain road, down a long snow-covered slope, come three MEN in white stealth like snowsuits, gliding catlike on snowboards, and seven MEN on skies in black behind them. The men remain in set positions, with firearms. The snowboarders schuss to a halt and survey the door. We see only the whites of their eyes. One of them bends and whisks away a few inches of powder, uncovering a buried detonator switch. Well away from the snowboarders, but above the door, we see and hear a muffled explosion. Snow flies everywhere, creating a rumbling, echoing avalanche.

Inside the mountain, in a high-tech "maximum-security" storage cave, a sleepy GUARD is awakened when he feels the cave shake. He checks the rows of surveillance screens in front of him. All is clear, except at the back entrance we first saw. He watches as the snow cascades off the side of the mountain to cover his Volvo and then obscures the camera from view. The screen fizzles and goes blank. "Avalanche!" the guard mumbles. "Scheiss! Mein Volvo …" He knows he'll be half a day digging his snowmobile out, so for now he blows it off, swivels in his chair, and starts playing a video game on another monitor, thinking, "It's just another day in the mountains."

The snowboarders have positioned themselves just above the door. One of them whacks the now broken surveillance camera with a wrench, then puts the tool away and takes a small package out of his backpack. It's a grenade. He pulls the pin, throws it down hard into the avalanched snow covering the door, and the snowboarders take cover. After the explosion, they look over the side and see that the snow has been cleared away. One by one, they drop over the side or the door and begin working on opening it.

Inside a plush suite in Jamaica, STAN WATSON (58, African American man) lies on his back, head under the kitchen sink, wrestling with a clogged garbage disposal. Stan's wife, BERTIE WATSON (56, attractive African American woman, caffe latte skin, pale green eyes) yells out, "Stan, let the hotel fix the disposal."

Stan's granddaughter, MATTIE EMORY (3, African American, large, happy eyes, a ready smile, and exploding curls), enters the kitchen, plops down, and plays with Stan's shoe.

Stan Watson is a handsome, four-star army general, the first African American to graduate No. 1 in his class at West Point, hero of the second Iraqi conflict, and the man who led the mission that captured SADDAM HUSSEIN and brought him to justice for war crimes, soon to be the president of the United States. Stan raises his head to see who is playing with his shoe and cracks his head on the disposal. He yells, "Ow!" rubbing his head, and smiles when he sees Mattie. He lifts her and then kisses her.

Meanwhile, inside the Swiss cave, the guard playing video games sees gas seeping under the door. He sniffs once, and then he's knocked out. The three snowboarders armed with portable computers enter, wearing oxygen masks. They take off their masks, exposing their faces. They are CAMERON SHAHERAZAD (46, a light-skinned African American man, with dreadlocks), Stan's GRANDSON (19, a light-complexioned African American man) and LOUIS SOLOMON (38, a Jewish man). Cameron ties up the guard in his chair. The others look for items as if they had cased the place already. On security monitors, we see laser beams in the hallways and in the vault.

Back at the Royal Caribbean Hotel in Jamaica, as Stan and the family head toward the beach, PEOPLE begin recognizing who he is, and the family is mobbed. People smile and wave and show much love and respect for Stan. Some ask for autographs, while others say how much they enjoyed his book. A MAN from New York offers to head up Stan's campaign, should he change his mind about running for president. Just as he has for months, Stan says he's making no plans.

Inside a vault in the storage cave, two of the snowboarders are rapidly taking digital pictures of documents. Just behind them, the other snowboarder is whistling loudly in admiration as he holds a heavy gold bar in both hands. The whole wall is lined with stacks of gold bricks. The two snowboarders taking pictures admonish him to put it back. One of them carefully places some documents and a small black book in plastic and puts them in his backpack.

Back in the surveillance room, the guard has woken up and has managed to push an alarm button on the wall with his toe. He laughs as he sees the snowboarders scramble on one of the surveillance screens, but he doesn't laugh long, because he loses his balance and falls backward onto the floor, "Scheiss, that hurts!"

In a ski chase through mountain passes, the snowboarders are chased by crack Swiss

SOLDIERS armed with military rifles. They are almost hit several times as they dodge bullets through perilous forest runs. Finally, as they come around a bend, one of the snowboarders pulls the pin on another grenade and tosses it at the mountain. There's an explosion above them, and a ton of snow comes down, forcing their pursuers to halt. The snowboarders laugh until they see that they've started another avalanche. One of the snowboarders who has been lagging behind reaches for another grenade but in his haste knocks something off his belt.

One of the pursuing military men makes it around the avalanche and discovers the fallen object. It's a geo-positioning device. He hears a rumble as the avalanche approaches and hurriedly skies into the forest to escape the tumbling snow.

Inside a nearby ski lodge, we see the Humpty Dumpty group members of Sigma Pi Phi, Alex Rutherford, Wilson Powers, Franklin Steadman, Floyd Davidson, Edna Addington, and PETER STRAUS (35, Swiss and Jewish) sitting around a table near a huge picture window, having hot toddies. One was a Black Panther, another, a famous defendant in a political trial. Some are playing chess, and all of them are trying to appear nonchalant and jovial, yet there's an undercurrent of nervousness in the group.

These members of Sigma Pi Phi have plotted something called "Operation Solid Assets." Alex gets up and looks outside. He sees the avalanche pouring down a ski run, and alerts the others. The group goes to the window to see, knowing they're safe.

On the way down the mountain, one of the young snowboarders struggles and falls. As he struggles to get back on his feet, he checks to see whether the gold bar is still in his backpack. He is in pain but jumps back on his board, and continues down the mountain with pursuers on skis not far behind.

As the air fills with snow from the onrushing avalanche, one of the pursuing skiers has just enough time to find the geo-positioning device dropped on the slopes and skis into the forest before the avalanche strikes. The snowboarding raider all make it, schussing out of the forest and into the ski village as the avalanche dwindles to nothing in the forest near the ski lodge.

The Egghead Gang hurriedly relocates to a nearby conference room and has a look at some documents captured during the bank heist. The snowboarders have brought back real documents, as well as some digitalized photos and a small leather-covered black book entitled, "LEONARDO DA VINCI CODEX, ALCHEMICAL PRACTICES." One photo projected on the wall draws gasps from a couple of the Egghead members. It is a shipping manifesto bearing a stamp from the federal government of the United States. It suggests that the United States, as well as foreign governments, banks, and some Fortune 500 companies were in the past actively involved in, and profiting from, gold and slave trading. If the rest of their research is right, it's the key they need to prove that one of the richest corporations in the United States, which is an international corporation today, made a lot of money long ago in the gold and slave trades, even though, all along, everyone thought the company's early millions came from textiles. That document and many others they pore over have tremendous international implications for governments and banks. They feel like celebrating but instead are quiet, as they consider the weight of what they have uncovered.

In the White House in Washington DC, PRESIDENT DAVID ABRAMS (48, Caucasian, moderately handsome) sits at his desk, as GENERAL ERNIE BEAUCHAMP (52, Caucasian, Marine general replacing Stan Watson) and SECRETARY OF STATE WARREN REDSTONE (62, Caucasian, slight man, thinning gray hair) enter. Within moments, CHIEF OF STAFF to the President, GENE RADAMIER (48, lean, recently divorced), enters saying, "President." The president says, "Thanks for coming, Gene, Ernie, Warren. Something's going on. Within minutes of each other, MARK TURNER at Ford, AL SMITH at AT&T, and JOHN WENTWORTH at Chevron called. Apparently, major segments of their company's assets have been frozen through accounts their corporations hold in Zurich."

The president continues his emergency meeting when the phone beeps. ELSIE EUBANKS, assistant to the president, interrupts his meeting. "Mr. President, President KROELLER is on the phone." The president asks, "President of Switzerland? Put him through, Elsie. President Kroeller, this is David Abrams." Kroeller says, "They have taken over the Bank Exchange. The security OFFICERS were released unharmed, the same situation with the Finance Ministry and the Bank Suisse D'International. It appears that they are well armed, with both explosives and computers, which is the way they have gained access. They apparently have all the security codes for the doors, vaults, and security systems." President Abrams asks, "Hostages?" Kroeller answers, "So far none.

None that we know of. They said they will contact us, and if we try to enter the buildings,
they will destroy them."

Meanwhile, back in Jamaica, Stan's family
is still not happy. They haven't made it to
the beach yet. Stan has insisted on a detour
through a Jamaican neighborhood to see the
rundown house where his father grew up. His
family stops complaining when they see the
conditions in which the tenants live. Then
they discover that they are related to these
people by blood, and the beach trip is forgotten. When they see his cousin, whose small
child is sick, Stan arranges for them to be
taken by taxi to a doctor. He secretly pays
the bill and has groceries delivered to their
home, leaving them an envelope of money.

Stan gets a call from the president of
the United States that his grandson is being
accused of spying for the United States and
was involved in the bank heist in Switzerland.
The president asks Stan to intervene.

Stan meets with the Swiss authorities and
his grandson is immediately released. A NEWS
REPORTER approaches Stan and his grandson when
they exit the prison, saying, "Mr. Watson is
it true that your grandson was involved in one
of the largest heists in Switzerland's history?" They ignore the reporters and enter a
limousine, which then drives off.

Stan delivers the boy to his PARENTS at a
hotel. They say they're staying behind another
day to wrap up some "loose ends" before they
head back to the United States. It's an "egghead thing that their friends all understand."
Stan's SON-IN-LAW says, "You will meet him at
the airport in a couple of days, right?" Stan
replies, "We'll be there." He turns to his

grandson and says, "Just in case, I've changed your flight to a UPS cargo jet. I want you to be safe. Too much is going on."

When Stan gets back to the United States, the president wonders out loud at a press conference whether Stan has reconsidered running for office. Stan declines politely. He tells the press that the incident in Switzerland was all a big misunderstanding.

A day later, Stan and his family see his grandson's UPS cargo jet descending as they stand in the arrivals terminal. They never get the chance to greet him because the plane explodes in the sky before it lands. Everyone screams.

At the White House in the cabinet room, President Abrams, Ernie Beauchamp, Warren Redstone, and Gene Radamier enter and take seats, as they gather for an emergency meeting. Alex Rutherford's face is already on the screen, with President Kroeller's face a smaller inset on the screen. On screen, Alex says, "We have seized vital assets and information of the United States and have successfully downloaded the information via satellite. We will return the Swiss facilities within twenty-four hours if you abide by the following conditions listed in our Manifesto, which we will present and explain to a representative of our choice. We have selected "General Stanley Watson."

Stan is intercepted by two Egghead members leaving his grandson's funeral. He is presented with a briefcase that has a laptop computer inside. Stan boots up and sees in quick succession a number of items listing where billions in illicit money came from and where it went to government leaders around the world both past and present. Included in those documents is the black bond book. Stan asks the Egghead Gang, "What is this?" They answer, "That's an important document. We will keep it in a maximum secure place and never show it to anyone. It's our ace in the hole."

After Stan is briefed on the demands of the Humpty Dumpty committee, he meets with the president of the United States and his staff. He says, "Well, that's it, sir." President Abrams asks Ernie, "General, what about the release of the Swiss facilities?" Ernie replies, "That already took place this morning. They are now in Swiss custody." Warren says, "But they still have control of our assets, and in effect tie up most of the World Bank funds."

After hearing about the conditions of the world and the hopelessness of people of color, and seeing evidence of oppression in government, Stan has a dream. A fire is blazing, but it's a big bonfire on a beach. Stan sees a black MAN on the beach. It's MARTIN LUTHER KING JR. and Stan doesn't know what to think about this. As he comes up to the bonfire, ghostly figures begin emerging from the nearby sea, and, as they walk toward the fire, the water evaporates from them rapidly, giving them an even more ghostly presence. They are in the costumes of their times: THURGOOD MARSHALL, CRAZY HORSE, HARRIET TUBMAN, MALCOLM X,

W. E. B. DUBOIS, DUKE ELLINGTON, SITTING BULL, FREDERICK DOUGLASS, and CÉSAR CHAVEZ, sitting on rocks around a bonfire. They speak to him then Stan awakes from his dream and says, "Bertie, I'm running for president."

Billboards, posters, and advertising signs saying "STAN WATSON FOR PRESIDENT" are plastered all over the city. Buses have on them

Stan's picture, which has a multicultural picture of the diversity of people at the top, the words, "CRY FREEDOM," then a picture of Stan standing in front of the American flag, and the words, "WE WILL STAND AS ONE." Stan speaks to the people, "America, cry freedom from the chains of oppression. I will tear down the barriers in our laws. We must break down the barriers in our lives, our minds, and in our hearts. We will stand as one."

The VILLAGERS of Freetown, in West Africa, and surrounding cities, gather and cheer the news—"Stan Watson is elected the new president"—as they watch a televised satellite from the Watson headquarters in the United States. In New York City we hear, "Ladies and gentlemen, we have a new president tonight. Winning by a landslide, President-elect Watson won the vote of the people, with 349 electoral votes. Yes, a new president. The Democrats have control of the House with 242 "seats". History has been made tonight. Our first African American President, Stan Watson."

Stan gets an idea for the "Forgotten People," a memorial he wants to build next to the Lincoln Memorial. He says his first priority is to get the ghost of slavery out of the psyche of the nation and heal racial differences. He feels a need to make right the inequality of U.S.history, and a monument to people who have been mistreated isn't a bad start. African slaves, Native Americans, even Chinese who helped build the transcontinental railroad can be included. Bertie reminds him to not forget women suffragettes who worked to gain the right to vote.

Weeks later, we're at the White House in the Oval Office, as "Hail to the Chief" plays

in the background. We see a photo of Nelson
Mandela, Stan with President Jimmy Carter,
Stan in a T-shirt standing with children in
front of a "Boys and Girls Club," photos of
President's Reagan and Clinton, Stan with
his command troops from Vietnam, drawings of
the Buffalo Soldiers from the civil war, the
Medal of Freedom, the Order of Jamaica, his
Eisenhower leadership prize, and a gleaming
sword collection from each branch of the military. Stan Watson is posing with his new cabinet as the PRESS takes pictures.

In the White House Diplomatic Reception
Room, Stan enters with SECRET SERVICE MEN,
as his GRANDCHILDREN Mattie, AMY, STEPHEN,
WILLIS, and DEXTER, enter with excitement,
hugging him. Stan says to Mattie, "My sweet
little granddaughter, how I love you so, and
all my grandchildren." Then Stan and the kids
enter the kitchen. The kitchen STAFF stands.
He says, "This is my granddaughter Mattie.
She'll be visiting here often." The kitchen
staff nod, with a slight smile.

After his grandchildren leave, Stan is meeting with Gene Radamier, his chief of staff,
in the Oval Office, when his assistant, Elsie,
interrupts them: "Mr. President, your call from
Zurich, sir." Stan and Gene listen on speakerphone to men from the Humpty Dumpty group
from the Swiss prison. Stan says, "Wilson,
Alex, how are things going? Gene is here with
me." Wilson say's "They could be a whole lot
worse and a whole lot better, Stan. Being in a
jail is still being in jail, even though it's
Swiss. What's going on with the job bill for
inner cities?" Gene replies, "We've run into
some snags. The gun and tobacco interests are
really flexing their muscles."

Meanwhile, AL SMITH, head of AT&T, who occasionally golfs with Stan, speaks to a SATELLITE SPECIALIST who is a spy: "So, what are you saying?" The satellite specialist answers, "Mr. Smith, it appears the Humpty Dumpties have figured out a way to change linkups and ID numbers after every call, and then essentially call forward the previously used number." Al says, "Brilliant, so no call records will leave a trail. How in the hell are they able to communicate from inside a Swiss jail?" The satellite specialist says, "I have no idea, sir." Al says, "Stay on it, and report to me directly. Here's my private pager and satellite number. If you can't reach me, here are the numbers for John Wentworth, head of Chevron, and Mark Turner at Ford. This is a joint project."

It's an early-morning tee time at the Burning Tree Golf Club, and Stan is playing golf with three of the most important CEOs in the nation. As they hit their tee shots, someone asks Stan what's first on his agenda. Stan says he's very interested in ending the historical residue of slavery and has been thinking over what it would take to make his people put it behind them forever. Of course, that's not something they've heard before and certainly not what they were expecting to hear from him. It makes some of them visibly nervous, and they think they don't have him under their thumb as they thought. The last CEO whiffs his tee shot, he's so nervous.

Stan and Bertie are comfortably snuggled in bed. Bertie says, "How does it feel after your first week as president?" Stan says, "It wouldn't feel half as good if you weren't here with me." He kisses her and she falls asleep.

Stan, dog-tired, looks over at a stack of papers on his desk, starts to get out of bed, and then changes his mind. Within seconds, he's asleep, and he dreams—the same beach, but a slightly different dream.

Stan walks along the beach until he comes to a circle of people. ABE LINCOLN now sits with Martin Luther King Jr., THOMAS JEFFERSON, Frederick Douglass, Crazy Horse, Harriet Tubman,W. E. B. Dubois, Sitting Bull, Cesar Chavez, and DUKE ELLINGTON playing keyboard. Stan says, "I am now president of the United States, now what?" W. E. B. Dubois says, "Stan, a talented tent of African Americans has a great obligation and responsibility to moti- vate, lead, and inspire the great underclass to achieve its full potential." Fredrick Douglass says, "You must do the things we wanted to do but could not." Then Martin Luther King Jr. stands, pulls out a large flaming piece of driftwood from the fire, and gives it to Stan.

He says, "The torch has been passed."

Outside a small local grocery store in East Oakland, California, STONE PAXTON (13, an African American boy), DRUG DEALER, has just made a transaction with a USER when a limou- sine pulls up. Stone walks up to the vehicle, not noticing that Secret Service vehicles are behind the limo. The window is lowered, reveal- ing Stan looking out. Stone says, "You're in luck today because I have a full range of asilic sebums. You want fast or slow?" Stan introduces himself, and then says, "And you are?" Stone replies, "Stone Paxton, because nothing hurts me."

A HOMELESS MAN and CHILDREN watch from a distance. Stan speaks into this boy's heart. Stone is touched by his words. His eyes well

up because no one has ever given this kid recognition. Stone says, "You see, Mr. President,
I can't read," and then lowers his head. Stan
says to him, "Stone, I need your help to change
all of this so that people are safe in their
beds at night, not afraid of being shot by a
stray bullet." Stan lifts his head. "Will you
help me?"

In the auditorium at East Middle School,
Oakland, CHILDREN and TEACHERS sit on bleachers waiting for the president to speak. Secret
Service agents are to the right and left of
the stage and stand at the entrance. Stan
talks with Stone Paxton, and then walks out on
stage. Stone turns, sticks his tongue out at
his friends, and claps quick and hard. Stan
says, "Thank you for having me here today.
You're right; you should have the best books
and computers to be able to get a good job. I
will see that your school is funded adequately
so that it will not close." The teachers and
children applaud.

In the Rose Garden, Bertie is conducting a press conference for the International
Conference on Women's Health & Human Rights.
Her little granddaughter Mattie is taking pictures but is a little bored listening to this
formal stuff, so she asks Alice, her mother,
if she may go see her grandfather. Alice says,
"Anything, bubby, but hurry back," and off
Mattie goes.

Stan is working alone in the Oval Office,
putting the finishing touches on his State of
the Union speech, when Mattie steps in. He's
reluctant at first, and then says he can give
her a few minutes. Mattie says she wants him
to take a picture of her sitting at his desk.
She wants to be president someday. She hands

him her camera and positions herself at the desk. Stan steps back into the center of the room to get just the right shot. Then the glass behind his desk shatters, and Mattie is shot through the back of the chair. She is killed instantly. Chaos ensues, with Secret Service men everywhere.

We hear SIRENS, as an ambulance and other emergency vehicles rush to the White House. The SOUND becomes indistinct, then muted. We hear MUSIC, "Auld Lang Syne (The Millennium Mix)," "The Essential," by Kenny G, over the scene. Broadcast on the TV and radio: "Breaking news: there has been an assassination attempt on the president tonight. Mattie Emory, the president's granddaughter, has been shot and killed." One of Stan's supporters watching the news at neighborhood bar says, "He kept his promise. He built a memorial for the forgotten people, created jobs, and took kids off the streets. Now this, why? They're trying to break him, push him out of office. You must fight for truth and righteousness. You are the bridge to freedom."

As REPORTERS wait, Stan comes out of the emergency room with blood on his shirt. He does a press conference right there, tears streaming down his cheeks, and says, "I will not rest until these cold-blooded killers have been brought to justice, whether it's a lone nut or an international cabal." Bertie and Alice stand there with him, tears rolling down their cheeks, but Alice's defiance and determination are awe-inspiring.

Inside the Oval Office, in the middle of the day, Stan sits in his chair, looking out the window. He's drinking Glenlivet, sipping it slowly, brooding and despondent. He takes a sip, and then throws the bottle across the room, where it shatters against the wall. He stands up in the window and screams outside, "Shoot now, god-dam it! Shoot me, you bastards!" Then, tears running down his cheeks, he repeatedly slams his fist into the wall by the window.

On a roundtable political discussion show like *This Week with Sam & Cokie,* the subject is the Watson administration. There's been another Cabinet resignation over a controversy that started up after the second honeymoon that resulted from Mattie's death wound down. The buzz around the White House is that President Watson is obsessing over whether the black militant who is the alleged perpetrator is the actual killer. They pontificate as we CUT TO …

Stan looks out the window from the Oval Office and sees DEMONSTRATORS carrying signs that read, "NAACP AND THE BLACK COALITION MARCH," repeatedly chanting, "Stan Watson took our jobs. Stan Watson took our jobs." Gene speaks to Bertie about Stan: "Bertie, you've got to do something. Stan has lost his focus. There is a vacuum, and I'm worried about what is filling it." Bertie replies, "I know. Either we do what we came here to do, or we should get out."

It's the Oprah Winfrey Show and OPRAH is interviewing Stan and Bertie about how the presidency is going. She asks if he's sure they want to do this, and they say yes. She's obviously nervous about something. So out of the wings come a beautiful white WOMAN and a teenage BOY who is Stan's illegitimate son. A Native American MAN watching the Oprah Show says, "They always try to find dirt, the

cutting board of man, now what?" Stan turns to
the boy, who is named THOMAS, and says, "I'm
sorry, son. I never wanted you to be exposed
to the world like this. I have always tried to
protect you."

A limousine and Secret Service vehicles
pull up in front of the Confederacy Bar in
North Carolina. We hear SIRENS, and then see
flashing lights. Several police cars enter the
scene. The police OFFICERS exit their vehicles and surround the building. The PEOPLE
inside look out and scramble for the exits,
ditching their drugs and illegal weapons,
but nobody can leave. Then RAYMOND sees that
it's the president and says, "He's here for
me. I sent the president an e-mail and told
him that I wasn't going to pay a damn dime
for any memorial or anything else." MELVIN
says, "Raymond, you threatened him." Raymond
insists, "No I didn't. I just told him …" BUCK
says, "You're a dead man. That was a threat."
Melvin says, "Here he comes, prizefighter. I
tell you you're toast, because he's mad." Stan
enters and asks, "Who is Raymond?" but no one
answers. Raymond is then pointed out and Stan
walks up to him. Raymond flippantly asks, "Did
you get my e-mail?" Then Stan says, "What did
you call me? Nigger!" Stan punches Raymond in
the face, and Raymond falls to the floor. Stan
picks him up and beats the living tar out of
him. We see that something is very wrong with
Stan.

Raymond's leg begins to shake violently,
and then he breaks down into hysterics.

"How do I get it out? How do I get out the
hate that my father fed me—the beatings, the
rapes? How do I get it out, the hatred in my
heart? He whipped me if I talked to the Jews.

He tied me up if I talked with the blacks. He said, 'Burn them.' He said that we were better, but we're nothing but poor white trash. How do I get out what's eating me inside, Stan? Help me." Everyone in the bar is shocked. Stan reaches out to Raymond, and like a small child who fell into a dark well. Stan says, "Raymond, you get it out with love."

Stan and Bertie are watching the evening news when they see breaking news come on. Stan's face is plastered across the TV screen. Bertie says, "Sometimes you do damn foolish things," and she turns off the TV. Stan pleads, "But honey, this was between love and hate … and love won. A man has been freed tonight." They lift their drinks and toast.

A SWAT TEAM surrounds a brick house in Washington DC. The team members break down the front door and enter. They search the rooms and then break down the basement door where they see pictures of the president's family on the wall and markings showing where and how the president would be killed. Weapons are confiscated. We hear Bertie talking over the scene: "This is a wake up call. We are in a war. Just because they caught the sniper doesn't change anything." Through a hidden door in the floor, the SWAT Team finds and handcuffs the SNIPER (45, Caucasian man), leading him upstairs and out of the house.

The next morning, Stan and Bertie have breakfast on the terrace of "The Lincoln Bedroom" at the White House to discuss the important matter of a new vice president. Stan chooses Dave Abrams, who was president prior to Stan's taking office. Bertie says, "Not after all those terrible things he said about you during the campaign. How could you trust him? He's a politician, Stan." But Stan has his reasons.

Stan has a conference call with members of the Egghead Group from prison. They tell him they've finally tracked down who was responsible for the bombing of the plane that carried Stan's grandson. Stan tells them his plan and why he has chosen Dave Abrams to be vice president.

Stan plays golf with the CEOs and tells them he's got the goods on them. He's also got their major personal bank accounts, with the transfers taking place while they were on their way to the club that morning. He lays out a list for them of big money guys and politicos who have shared in illegal loot of all kinds over the years, and how it's been tracked down, almost to the penny. "Don't take it personal, boys," he says. "It's just business. And if all this doesn't work …" He holds up the codex.

Gene is being chased by a black car with tinted windows. He dodges the vehicle several times when another car hits it, freeing him. SPECTATORS drive slowly because of the car nearly hanging off the bridge. We hear sirens and then see POLICE.

Then, a few nights later, a POLICE cruiser approaches a parked car. The OFFICER (32, Hispanic man) looks and sees a MAN asleep. When he approaches the vehicle, he finds the man, Chief of Staff Gene Radamier, shot in the head, dead. On the radio we hear, "Chief of Staff Gene Radamier was found dead late last night. He was shot and killed at Potomac Park, where police found his body. Radamier was recently divorced, and his death is being considered a possible suicide, but an investigation is …"

Then, at Gene's funeral, his ex-wife, SUSAN RADAMIER, whispers, "Gene didn't kill himself, Bertie. He was murdered." Stan watches David when he looks at the coffin, then back at him and Bertie, because David is thinking, "You're next."

In the computer lab at Lincoln Elementary School in Oakland, Stan, the Secret Service, kids HERSHELL and ANTHONY, and the PRINCIPAL, are shocked when they see all the equipment trashed. On the walls are spray-painted messages: "Impede, Shackles, Fetters, Manacles," and "THE CHAINS OF OPPRESSION WILL REMAIN." Anthony insists on speaking to the president alone. In the limo, he says, "Mr. President, I received a phone call last night from Wilson Powers. He said he couldn't contact you directly anymore and to tell you that John, Al, and Mark are the 'we.' He also said to tell you that you must move very quickly."

In the Watson home in Arlington, Virginia, RODNEY and WILBUR, dressed as FBI agents, walk up to the front door. They look through the windows and, seeing no one, they disarm the electronic security system and enter. A NEIGHBOR, drawn to the window by a noise, sees the two men enter Stan's house, and she calls the police.

Stan, Mark, Al, and John have a serious meeting over drinks on the terrace at the Burning Tree Golf Club, while sneaky business is occurring at Stan's home. Rodney looks through the drawers and then checks the front of the refrigerator, looking for information. His search is quick and precise. Wilbur looks through papers and a date book on the desk. By the look on his face, he has found something. He holds a flight schedule. He hears a police

SIREN. "Following him out, running down the stairs to the living room, Wilbur says, "They may be headed for Jamaica."

Officer's arrived and open fire directly at Rodney, killing him. Wilbur fires wounding Kinney, and they roll on the floor. Officer LIGHTFOOT manages to kick the gun out of Wilbur's hand, but Wilbur expertly wriggles out of Kinney's grasp and disappears through the front door.

The rising sun shines on Bertie's face as MARIETTA rushes in to wake her and Alice in the bedroom of Marietta's home in Jamaica. "Wake up, Bertie, Alice. I just spoke with Stan. They know you're here. We have to hide you somewhere else. Hurry, get dressed," says Marietta. Bertie and Alice dress and throw clothes in their suitcases. "Hurry, go out the back. There will find a shed and a trap door that leads to a tunnel. It will take you to the street. Somebody will be waiting for you to take you to the airport." They hug, and Bertie and Alice rush out. Within minutes, Wilbur kicks down the front door. "I know they've been here. I'll burn this shack to the ground with you in it, old woman," he says as he holds Marietta by the throat, lifting her off the floor.

Meanwhile, in the Oval Office, Stan sits at his desk typing on the computer. "Plan B, everyone. Initiate Humpty Dumpty on the Board of Directors at Chevron, AT&T, and Ford." In a prison cell in Geneva, Alex Rutherford sits in an isolated room with a PRISON GUARD standing at the door with his back to him. Alex sends a message on a small laptop computer. He types, "Hershell, are you there? I have the bank and stock account numbers. Are you ready

to receive?" Hershell sits at a computer communicating with Alex. We see Alex's message on
his computer screen. He types, "Ready."

REPORTERS swarm around the exit where
SPECTATORS holding the American flag cheer and
wave as the Egghead Group—Alex Rutherford,
Peter Straus, Wilson Powers, Franklin Steadman,
Floyd Davidson, Edna Addington, Cameron Ameron,
Shaherazad Haherazad, Louis Uouis Solomon, and
Rishad Ali exit. NEWS REPORTER #3 (African
American man), says, "Alex Rutherford, the
Humpty Dumpties have been exonerated, and you
are all now heroes. How does it feel being
responsible for bringing down the man who
bombed the plane, killing the President's
grandson?" Alex says, "Truth has set us free
and has chained our adversary. The taste of
freedom is sweet."

Bertie and Alice enter the Watson residence
in the White House with suitcases and set them
down in the foyer. Stan glides in and embraces
them. He says, "Thank God, my girls are safe."
He turns to Bertie and says, "My sweet love,
how I adore you." He takes Bertie by the hands
and dances with her; he spins her and then
does a dip saying, "I have something to tell
you. Sit, my dear. I'll be right back." He
goes back to the foyer where Alice is standing and touches her face. "My baby, you are my
treasure. I am so sorry, honey, about Mattie.
She will never be forgotten." Her eyes well
up. "Dad …" Stan softly says, "No. You mean
so much to me. Honey, you will have another
child. Who knows, maybe twins. Someone is here
to see you. Forgive him, baby." They hug, and
Stan kisses her on the cheek. Then he dances
her to the bedroom door, where she sees her
HUSBAND, from whom she has been separated.

Alice enters the bedroom. They cry, embrace, and kiss.

Stan closes the door and enters the living room. He sits in a chair in front of Bertie and takes her hand. He says, "I found something." Bertie says, "What?" He tells her about his life in a way that he never has before. "When I was a boy, we were poor. I wanted to help my parents, so I climbed a mango tree that was in our backyard and threw down the mangos so I could sell them. Then I lost my balance and fell through the outhouse into the sewage. I was stuck there up to my neck. I screamed out to my father. He came outside, saw me, and punished me by leaving me there all day. That pit of sewage was a place of horror, and in the darkness, I cried. From that time on, when I was lonely or hurt, I locked myself in the closet, punishing myself as my father did. Then I decided to have a heart of stone so no one could hurt me. Remember me telling you about the boy, Stone Paxton? Well, that was me. I wasn't selling drugs, I just had a bad attitude and felt unloved. And when Stone said, 'you see, Mr. President, I can't read' "I could read, I just couldn't read into the hearts of those around me. Then he touched my face and said, 'Stone, I need your help to change all of this, so that people are safe in their beds at night, not afraid of being shot by a stray bullet. Will you help me?' I knew I was a part of him, that he had love for me. He cared in a way no one ever has, and, in my mind, he would be my father, a father of hope. So I held him near to my heart, and I stopped locking myself in a closet, crying, feeling forgotten, and I promised I would never forget 'the Forgotten People.' And that day, when

the first black president made a speech at my
school, I knew that would be me. From that
moment on, I fought for love. I knew I would
find it, so I could give it to the world. My
suffering became my stone, the one I would
stand upon and build from there. When the
boy, Stone Paxton, said, 'I was sorry to hear
about your granddaughter,' it was as if I knew
my own destiny but could not stop what would
happen."

Alice and her husband stand in the doorway
as tears come down. They enter, and then sit.
Bertie asks, "So the president really wasn't
there?" Stan answers, "Right, just a boy who
found hope. After he touched my heart, I was
free from the chains of despair and poverty.
He enriched me, giving me hope to aspire, and
I did. Do you understand? What I aspired to be
became my hope; it came to life, the president.
Then Stone Paxton disappeared like a cloud
in the wind. Then, as a man, I started having dreams, dreams of heroes, those who have
touched the world with greatness. I dreamed of
my father the way I wanted him to be, a man
of God, a man of strength and hope. And in my
despair, I would dream a place of darkness,
and my dreams empowered me. Bertie, I found
the missing piece. I am the father of many,
and the people are my children. None will be
forgotten." Bertie says in awe, "Stan ..." Alice
says, "Dad, what an incredible story."

Stan hands Bertie a sealed envelope. Bertie
asks, "What's this?" She opens the envelope, "A paternity test?" Stan confesses, "I
was never unfaithful to you. Not even for a
moment. In our troubled time, I met a young
pregnant woman who wanted to die. She did not
want to carry the shame alone, so I vowed she

could say that I was Thomas's father." Alice
asks, "Why didn't you tell the people?" He
says, "Should I crucify him so that I may
be free and let him carry the shame? No,
therefore I will die with the truth so he is
spared. He was forgotten by his father but
not by me."

He finishes with, "I stand against the bullet of defeat. I am no longer a boy with a
stone heart but a man full of love. I stand
for the poor and the hungry. I will be a
shield against injustice. I do not stand for
the system. It was the system that oppressed
the people. Therefore in my suffering I cried
freedom, and I took my cries to the people of
the world."

In the White House East Room, the president
holds a press conference. A REPORTER asks,
"Mr. President, is it true that Vice President
David Abrams, and corporate heads Al Smith,
Mark Turner, and John Wentworth were the mas-
terminds of your grandson's, Mattie's, and
Gene Radamier's murders?" In a police sta-
tion, David Abrams, Al Smith, Mark Turner, and
John Wentworth are handcuffed, numbered, and
photographed.

Near the Lincoln Memorial, flags encircle
a beautiful monument. Which has four walls
with equal entrances that divide them. Each
wall has countless pictures of PEOPLE on it.
In the center are statues of an ethnic diversity of people, including children gathered
together. There are no people in sight until
Stan speaks. SLOW PAN over title on wall, "THE
FORGOTTEN PEOPLE," then over the pictures on
the wall, then the title below the pictures,
"You will never be forgotten. You are stars in
the night." Stan, Bertie, their grandchildren,

and Alice and her husband, stand on stage with
Secret Service all around.

Unknown to Stan, PEOPLE are grouped by race
outside the monument. As he speaks, they enter
and come together as one, hugging, kissing, and
smiling at each other. Thousands gather. Stan
says, "We shall overcome prejudices, racial
conflict, division, and conquer hate with love,
and violence with peace. We shall overcome. We
shall overcome poverty with generosity, coldness of heart with warmth, hunger with sharing. We will be blameless toward one another
because we stand as one. We shall overcome.
We thank Abe Lincoln, Martin Luther King Jr.,
Nelson Mandela, Malcolm X, Thurgood Marshall,
Crazy Horse, Harriet Tubman, W. E. B. Dubois,
Frederick Douglass, César Chavez, and countless more. They laid the stones to the crossing of the bridge to freedom."

Then we see the boy, Stone Paxton, wave
at Stan. Stan winks and smiles, and then
Stone disappears. Fireworks go off. Then Stan
shouts, "Yes we can," seven times, with his
arms toward the sky, then the people also
shout "Yes We Can." It's truly a historic
moment. The people ROAR as Stan steps down,
shaking hands. He and his family exit. Then
MUSIC, "The Humpty Dumpty," plays, and Stan,
his family, and the people that the audience
recognizes follow him out, dancing. Then all
the people dance.

Stan and Bertie cuddle in the back of a
limo. MUSIC plays in the limo: the "Beige
Movement" from Duke Ellington's *Black, Brown,
and Beige.* Stan says, "All I ever wanted is
sitting right next to me. I love you, Bertie."
They kiss. "I'm the president. We can do anything we want." Bertie says, "Anything?" He

says, "Within reason. I'm an old guy, you know." She says, "Come here, you old guy. My hero."

Stan and Bertie in the limo, taking in Capitol Hill, enjoying the energy of Washington lit up at night, with the new memorial prominent.

As the credits roll, the NARRATOR says, "In Recognition of the human desire and spirit to exercise self-determination, and to pursue life, liberty, and happiness. Because of historical facts and events, let us put into context and perspective that we hold these truths to be self-evident and relevant, that "all men" were created equal. But because of certain inherent characteristics, they were not allowed the same opportunity to pursue their dreams and fulfill their destinies to exploit their fullest potential in achieving all that they were ordained and destined to have for themselves and their offspring. They had the right to freedom then, you have the right to freedom now and in the future. You have the right to collect for your ancestors everything that's owed to them, and to use and invest these assets for your progeny into perpetuity, and to pass on your history, culture, traditions, knowledge, wealth, and family spirit. This is a fundamental right every people possesses. To this end, we have established a fund of five trillion dollars in gold, in a numbered Swiss account, code name 'the Twenty-first century Project.' These funds are for education, the uplifting and elevation of your massive underclass, and to ensure that all the nations in the "New World Order" survive through the twenty-first century. The Codex is a book of alchemy containing the formula for turning baser metals into gold: "Yes We Can" and "Yes We Did."

"THE PRESIDENT"

"THE EPPIEOLOGIST"

Original Screenplay (1997)

By

Epaphroditus ("Eppie") Elkahan

Epaphroditus ("Eppie") Elkahan
Island Productions/Cry Freedom Pictures
www.cryfreedompictures.com
cryfreedompictures@yahoo.com
PO Box 574
Pacific Grove, CA 93950
917-456-2194

FADE IN:

EXT. HARVARD UNIVERSITY - NIGHT

The campus is quiet and still except for a light in the African American Studies Department.

INT. AFRICAN AMERICAN STUDIES DEPARTMENT, HARVARD - NIGHT

ALEX STUART RUTHERFORD (46, African American man, Department Chairman), WILSON RUSTIN POWERS (60, African American man), FRANKLIN JUNIUS STEADMAN (43, African American man) and FLOYD KVAMME DAVIDSON (45, African American man), all members of Sigma Pi Phi, sit at a confer- ence table, each looking through papers, as EDNA SESSIONS ADDINGTON a.k.a. "EDY," (42, African American beauty) walks around the table. The Humpty Dumpty members are always in black attire and wear sunglasses.

MALE NARRATOR (V.O.)
Members of Sigma Pi Phi, code name "HUMPTY DUMPTY," secretly meet.

Reviewing the papers, the members nod their heads.

EDNA
Gentlemen, this plan will provide
the educational, economical,
social, political, and ethical
foundation to prepare us for the
twenty-first century.

WILSON
But—

EDNA
But what, Wilson? Where will the
Money come from?

                                        CUT TO:

EXT. ROAD, MT. DUFOURSPITZE, SWISS ALPS - DAY

ON SCREEN: SWISS ALPS

In the dead of winter, we see a high alpine
road that dead-ends at an armored entrance
door on the side of Mt. Dufourspitze. A high-
tech, high-concept Volvo snowmobile is parked
against a stone fence nearby.

Above the door, a surveillance TV camera swivels back and forth, surveying the area.

Above the mountain road, down a long snow-
covered slope, come three SNOWBOARDERS in
white stealthlike snowsuits, wearing white
ski masks, gliding catlike on snowboards, and
seven MEN on skies in black behind them. The
Men remain in set positions with firearms. The
Snowboarders schuss to a halt and survey the
door. We see only the whites of their eyes.

One of them bends and whisks away a few inches
of powder, uncovering a buried detonator
switch.

Well away from the Snowboarders, but above the
door, we SEE and HEAR a muffled explosion. Snow
flies everywhere, creating a rumbling, echoing
avalanche.

                                        CUT TO:

EXT. BANK SUISSE D' INTERNATIONAL, SWISS ALPS
- MORNING

We see the bank and surrounding closed
stores.

INT. BANK SUISSE D' INTERNATIONAL,
SURVEILLANCE ROOM - MORNING

In a high-tech, maximum-secured cave, GUARD
(55, Caucasian, pudgy man) sitting in a chair
with his legs on the desk is awakened when he
feels the cave shake.

He checks the rows of surveillance screens in
front of him. All is clear, except at the back
entrance we first saw. He watches as the snow
cascades off the side of the mountain, covering his Volvo and obscuring the camera from
view. The screen fizzles and goes blank.

GUARD
(Softly)
Avalanche! Scheiss! Mein Volvo.

He shrugs his shoulders, swivels in his chair,
and starts playing a video game on another
monitor. To him, it's another day in the
mountains.

EXT. BANK SUISSE D' INTERNATIONAL, SWISS ALPS
MORNING

Near the back entrance of the bank, the three
Snowboarders have positioned themselves just
above the door. One of them whacks the broken
surveillance camera with a wrench, then puts
the tool away and takes a small object out of

his backpack. It's a grenade. He pulls the pin, throws it down hard into the avalanched snow covering the door. They take cover.

After the explosion, they look over the side and see that the snow has been cleared away. One by one, they drop over the side and begin working on opening the door.

                                        CUT TO:

EXT. BANK/LE MINISTERE DE FINANCE, ZURICH - MORNING

Seven MEN in ski masks, wearing black protective gear, holding firearms, run toward the bank.

                                        CUT TO:

EXT. BANK/EXCHANGE DE SUISSE, ZURICH - MORNING

Seven MEN IN ski masks, wearing black protective gear, holding firearms, run toward the bank.

                                        CUT TO:

EXT. ROYAL CARIBBEAN HOTEL, JAMAICA - MORNING

ON SCREEN: JAMAICA

It's a beautiful morning as the sun rises on the distant ocean near the hotel.

INT. ROYAL CARIBBEAN HOTEL, JAMAICA, WATSON SUITE- MORNING

In a plush suite, STAN WATSON (58, African American man), lies on his back, head under the kitchen sink, wrestling with a clogged garbage disposal.

Stan's wife, BERTIE WATSON (56, attractive African American woman, café latte skin, pale green eyes) yells out –

BERTIE (O.S.)
Stan, let the hotel fix the disposal.

Stan's granddaughter, MATTIE EMORY (3, African American, large, happy eyes, a ready smile, and exploding curls) enters the kitchen, plops down, and plays with Stan's shoe.

MALE NARRATOR (V.O.)
Stan Watson, four-star army general. First African American to
Graduate No. 1 in his class at West Point.

Stan raises his head to see who is playing with his shoe and cracks his head on the disposal.

STAN
Ow.

Rubbing his head, Stan smiles when he sees Mattie. He lifts her up, and then kisses her.

MALE NARRATOR (V.O.)
Hero of the second Iraqi conflict and the man who led the mission that captured Saddam Hussein and brought him to justice for war crimes. Soon to be the president.

ON SCREEN TITLE: YES WE CAN

CUT TO:

INT. BANK SUISSE D'INTERNATIONAL,
SURVEILLANCE ROOM - MORNING

The guard playing video games sees gas seeping
under the door. He sniffs once, and then he's
knocked out.

The three Snowboarders, armed with portable
computers, enter wearing oxygen masks. CAMERON
SHAFERAZAD (46, a light-complexioned African
American man, with dreadlocks)Stan's GRANDSON
(19, a light-complexioned African American
man), and LOUIS SOLOMON (38, Jewish man).
Cameron ties up the guard in his chair. The
others look for items as if they have cased
the place already.

On security monitors, we see laser beams in
the hallways and in the vault.

Cameron enters codes into the security monitor
that shut off security devices, allowing them
to enter several doors.

Cameron's mobile phone BEEPS.

CAMERON
(Into phone)
Twenty-two. Yes, we're in. No, just started.
Copy that. 0300 check in.

INT. BANK SUISSE D'INTERNATIONAL, SWISS ALPS
- MORNING

Moving with precision, men from the team go
from security station to station, tying up the

chloroformed GUARDS, who are on the floor, and then loading them into mail carts, which they push into an open elevator that is heading to the basement.

INT. BANK SUISSE D'INTERNATIONAL, BASEMENT, SWISS ALPS - MORNING

Stan's grandson and a MAN in black, wearing a black mask, exit the elevator and wheel a load of unconscious guards to air vents, propping them up so they will breathe uncontaminated air. Stan's grandson's mobile phone BEEPS.

STAN'S GRANDSON
(Into phone)
Twenty-three. We're in. Talk to you at 0300.

CUT TO:

INT. ROYAL CARIBBEAN HOTEL, LOBBY, JAMAICA - MORNING

Stan, his wife Bertie, and his daughter ALICE EMORY (32, eloquent), who holds her daughter Mattie, head to the beach. When PEOPLE recognize him, the family is mobbed.

ADMIRER #1 (38, Caucasian man wearing suit) works his way through the crowd. People smile, wave, showing love and respect. Stan and his family acknowledge them. Some ask for an autograph.

ADMIRER #1
Stan Watson, right? Loved your book.
(shakes Stan's hand)
What an honor. Men like you shape the world.

(nods to Bertie)
Mrs. Watson

Admirer #1 departs when ADMIRER #2 (45, Caucasian businessman) approaches Stan.

ADMIRER #2
(shakes Stan's hand)
From New York, sir. Should you change your mind, love to head up
your campaign. Running for president?

Bertie looks at Stan.

STAN
I'm making no plans.

                                        CUT TO:

INT. BANK SUISSE D'INTERNATIONAL, CENTRAL SECURITY - MORNING

Stan's grandson, wearing oxygen mask, taps in computer messages.

STAN'S GRANDSON
Daytime air-conditioning system activated. Elevating the air exchange rate.

Cameron, also wearing an oxygen mask, enters and tests the air with a digital air analyzer.

CAMERON
Five, four, three, two, one.

They both look at their watches and remove their oxygen masks. Stan's grandson taps in further commands, and the door to the safety deposit vault opens.

STAN'S GRANDSON
(Excited)
Yeah, baby!

Louis enters the scene, and his mobile unit BEEPS.

LOUIS
(into phone)
Twenty-four. Humpty dumpty, things are looking good. Check you at
0300.

                                    CUT TO:

EXT. /INT. WATSONS' CAR, JAMAICAN NEIGHBORHOOD - MORNING

Stan drives his family in a BMW 760 series through a rundown Jamaican neighborhood. Bertie gently rubs Stan's neck. Alice and Mattie sit in the back dressed for the beach.

ALICE
Dad, I thought we were going to the beach. Why are we driving through this dump?

Stan is slightly annoyed with his daughter's comment.

BERTIE
Alice, dumps are for garbage. People with little money are poor,
and maybe if you had had a taste of it, your mouth would not be so bitter.

STAN
This is where I grew up.
(eyes welling up)

ALICE
(Lowering head)
I'm sorry, Dad.

                                        CUT TO:

INT. FESTOONIE HOME, LIVING ROOM, JAMAICA
- MORNING

RUTH FESTOONIE (32, African American, sickly,
coughing) cries out for help on her knees,
before her sick, crying TODDLER, who is lying
on the couch in the middle of a filthy, poverty-stricken home.

RUTH
(Weeping)
Help me, Father. Please send us help.

She cries into the belly of her child.

                                        CUT TO:

INT. BANK SUISSE D'INTERNATIONAL, VAULT,
SWISS ALPS - MORNING

Cameron, Louis, and Stan's grandson enter.
With a set of double keys, Cameron extracts
several drawers and boxes. The men quickly
open the drawers and boxes, keeping documents,
keys, videos, audio cassettes, and artifacts
separated.

They are rapidly taking digital pictures of documents. Stan's grandson whistles loudly in admiration as he holds a heavy gold bar in both hands. The whole wall is lined with stacks of gold bricks.

CAMERON
(To Stan's grandson)
Don't even think about it.

LOUIS
The one with the gold never makes it out. Put it back.

Cameron carefully places some documents and a small black leather book in plastic and puts them in his backpack.

                                              CUT TO:

EXT./INT. WATSONS' CAR, JAMAICAN NEIGHBORHOOD - MORNING

Stan is looking for an address in a poverty-stricken neighborhood when he sees MARIETTA (80, a thin African American woman) standing in an open doorway. He slows the car to a stop.

STAN
Excuse me. I'm trying to find 102 Elkahan Street.

MARIETTA
Whose house?

Stan exits the car and walks up to Marietta.

STAN
My father's home as a child.

MARIETTA
His name?

STAN
Watanabe. Ernesto Watanabe.

MARIETTA
(Pointing)
Over there. Belongs to Ernesto.

Marietta slowly walks down her front porch
with Stan. He waves for Bertie to join them.
Marietta, Stan, and Bertie cross a dirt road
to the Festoonie home.

EXT. FESTOONIE HOME, JAMAICA - MORNING

Stan, Bertie, and Marietta stand at the front
door, which is a canvas flap. The paint is peel-
ing from the house, the yard is not kept, and
an old broken-down car is in the driveway.

MARIETTA
(Yelling)
Festoonie, you got visitors.
(turns to Stan)
May be in the fields.

Then we hear a voice from inside the house.

RUTH (O.S.)
Come in, Marietta. I'm in here.

Marietta, Bertie, and Stan enter the Festoonie
home.

INT. FESTOONIE HOME, LIVING ROOM, JAMAICA
- DAY

Poverty smells, but what Stan sees hurts him.
The furniture torn and broken, floors worn down
almost to the dirt, and debris everywhere.
Bertie looks at Stan.

MARIETTA
Ruth, this man claims to be Ernesto Watanabe's
son.

RUTH
What's your name?

STAN
Stan Watson, and this is my wife, Bertie.

BERTIE
Hi.

STAN
My father lived here as a boy until he was
six. Then they joined my grandfather, who came
to the States before them to find work.

Ruth
Then we're related. My grandparents were your
father's cousins.

STAN
Cousins, amazing. What a small world!

MARIETTA
Ruth, why are you home?

RUTH

Me and the baby are sick.
(coughs)
Just couldn't go out there today. So Rever
went alone.

The baby cries, fidgeting.

STAN
Want us to take you to the doctor?

Ruth and Marietta look at each other and
smile.

MARIETTA
Stan, there are no doctors around here. And if
there were, they would be too expensive.

STAN
(looking at Bertie)
We'll get you help.

Stan's cell phone RINGS. Stan turns and answers
the phone.

STAN (CONT'D)
(on cell phone)
Watson.

ELSIE EUBANKS (45, Caucasian, plain), Assistant
to the president, devoted to his political
career, contacts Stan.

ELSIE (O.S.)
Mr. Watson, Elsie Eubanks. A call from the
president, sir.

STAN
(to Bertie)

The president …

Marietta and Ruth mouth "The president," as Stan and Bertie exit the house.

CUT TO:

INT. BANK SUISSE D'INTERNATIONAL,
SURVEILLANCE ROOM, SWISS ALPS – DAY

The guard wakes up and manages to push an alarm button on the wall with his foot. He laughs as he sees Cameron, Louis, and Stan's grandson scramble on one of the surveillance screens. In a tilted chair, he falls backward onto the floor.

GUARD
Scheiss, that hurts!

                                    CUT TO:

EXT. BANK/EXCHANGE DE SUISSE, ZURICH - DAY

The rest of the team in snowsuits and masks
enters a helicopter, which looks military, but
is not. It lifts off.

                                    CUT TO:

INT. DOCTOR'S OFFICE, JAMAICA - DAY

DOCTOR DELORES SANCHEZ (34, Hispanic) shakes
down a thermometer and sticks it into Ruth's
mouth, as the toddler sits in a chair playing
with a toy.

                                    CUT TO:

EXT. WHITE HOUSE, WASHINGTON DC - DAY

FULL SHOT OF THE WHITE HOUSE.

INT. WHITE HOUSE, OVAL OFFICE, WASHINGTON DC
- DAY

PRESIDENT DAVID ABRAMS (48, Caucasian, moderately handsome) sits at his desk as GENERAL
ERNIE BEAUCHAMP (52, Caucasian, Marine General
replacing Stan Watson) and SECRETARY OF STATE
WARREN REDSTONE (62, Caucasian, slight man,
thinning gray hair) enter.

Within moments, CHIEF OF STAFF to the president,

GENE RADAMIER (48, lean, recently divorced), enters.

GENE
President.

The men nod as the president calls each of their names.

PRESIDENT
Thanks for coming, Gene, Ernie, Warren. Something's going on. Within minutes of each other, Mark Turner at Ford, Al Smith at AT&T, and John Wentworth at Chevron called.

ERNIE
Mr. President?

PRESIDENT
Apparently, major segments of their companies' assets have been frozen through accounts their corporations hold in Zurich.

                                    CUT TO:

EXT. FESTOONIE HOME, JAMAICA - DAY

A taxi cab enters the scene. Ruth and her child begin to exit when the CAB DRIVER (58, Caucasian man) rushes to her door.

RUTH
How much? Do I owe you?

CAB DRIVER
(smiling)
It's been taken care of.

RUTH
(whispering)
Like the doctor …
INT. FESTOONIE HOME, KITCHEN, JAMAICA - DAY

Ruth gasps when she walks into the kitchen. She sees numerous bags of groceries on the counter and the floor. Then she sees an envelope, picks it up with shaking hands, and opens it. Ten one-hundred-dollar bills are inside. Tears of joy.

RUTH
That man is an angel.

                                    CUT TO:

EXT. MT. DUFOURSPITZE, SWISS ALPS - DAY

In a ski chase through mountain passes, Cameron, Louis, and Stan's grandson are chased by five crack Swiss SOLDIERS armed with military rifles. The men are almost hit several times as they dodge bullets along perilous forest runs.

Finally, as they come around a bend, Stan's grandson pulls the pin on another grenade and tosses it at the mountain.

There's an explosion above them, and a ton of snow comes down, forcing their pursuers to halt.

They laugh, until they see that they've started another avalanche. Stan's grandson, who has been lagging behind, reaches for another grenade, but, in his haste, he knocks something off his belt.

One of the pursuing military men makes it around the avalanche and discovers the fallen object. It's a geo-positioning device. He hears a rumble as the avalanche approaches, then hurriedly skies into the forest to escape the tumbling snow.

The men think they are safe when they don't see the military behind them and see a ski lodge before them.

CUT TO:

INT. WHITE HOUSE, OVAL OFFICE, WASHINGTON DC - DAY

The president is still meeting with his head people.

WARREN
Mr. President, I thought all American-based corporations' reserves were held in the US.

PRESIDENT
It gets worse, Warren. Dave Eubanks at Treasury tells me that much of our gold reserves are also held there.

ERNIE
Aren't they at Ft. Knox and Ft. Henry?

PRESIDENT
About half. The other half has been accumulated in Zurich.

WARREN
How long has that been the case?

PRESIDENT
We started transferring contingency funds
there in the Nixon era and have been steadily
adding to them over the years. Most of them
are tied into interlocking accounts with other
countries and the IMF in Brussels.

ERNIE
The World Bank again. Jesus Christ.

                                    CUT TO:

INT. SKI LODGE, MT. DUFOURSPITZE, SWISS ALPS
- DAY

Sigma Pi Phi members Alex Rutherford, Wilson
Powers, Franklin Steadman, Floyd Davidson,
Edna Addington, and PETER STRAUS (35, Swiss
and Jewish) sit around a table near a huge
picture window, drinking hot toddies.

Some are playing chess, and all of them are
trying to appear nonchalant and jovial, yet
there's an undercurrent of nervousness in the
group.

MALE NARRATOR (V.O.)
Members of Sigma Pi Phi have plotted something called Operation Solid Assets. One was a
Black panther, another a famous defendant in
a political trial.

Alex gets up and looks outside. He sees the
avalanche pouring down a ski run, and alerts
the others.

ALEX

Look! An avalanche.

The group goes to the window to see, knowing they're safe.

CUT TO:

INT. WHITE HOUSE, OVAL OFFICE, WASHINGTON DC - DAY

The president continues his emergency meeting when the phone BEEPS. Elsie Eubanks, assistant to the president, interrupts his meeting.

ELSIE (O.S.)
(on speakerphone)
Mr. President, President KROELLER is on the phone.

PRESIDENT
President of Switzerland? Put him through, Elsie. President Kroeller, this is David Abrams.

CUT TO:

EXT. Mt. DUFOURSPITZE, SWISS ALPS - DAY

Stan's grandson falls. Before getting up, he checks to see if the gold bar is still in his backpack. He struggles to get back on his feet. In pain, he jumps back on his skies and continues down the mountain, with the military not far behind.

The air fills with snow from the onrushing avalanche. The members of the military ski into the forest before the avalanche strikes.

Cameron, Louis, and Stan's grandson make it, schussing out of the forest and into a ski village as the avalanche dwindles to nothing in the forest near the ski lodge.

                                   CUT TO:

INT. SKI LODGE, MT. DUFOURSPITZE, SWISS ALPS - DAY

PEOPLE warm themselves around the fireplace; others shake off the snow from skiing. Cameron, Louis, and Stan's grandson enter. Cameron hands Edna the plastic bag containing papers, pictures, and the black book. Then they quickly exit.

INT. SKI LODGE, CONFERENCE ROOM, SWISS ALPS - DAY

Edna removes the contents of the plastic bag as Alex, Wilson, Floyd, Franklin, and Peter sit around a table.

We see that the black book's title is: "Leonardo da Vinci Codex of Alchemical Practices."

EDNA
Gentlemen, we may have just entered what future historians will call the Postmodern Reconstruction Period.

Edna sets up equipment and on a TV monitor appears:
SLAVE CARGO SHIPPING MANIFESTO - 1802 UNITED STATES FEDERAL FRIGATE "AMERICAN LIBERTY"; PORT OF CALL: SAVANNAH

Everyone gasps at the implications.

WILSON
Edy, you may be right.

EDNA
Peter, tell them what this is.

PETER STRAUS
It's a shipping manifesto bearing a stamp from the federal government of the United States. It suggests that U.S. and foreign banks, and some Fortune 500 companies, were actively involved in, and profiting from, gold and slave trading.

FLOYD
Yes, it's the key we need to prove that one of the richest corporations in the US, which is an international corporation today, made a lot of money long ago in the trading of gold and slaves.

ALEX
Even though everyone thought the company's early millions came from textiles.

EDNA
Gentlemen, we hit the jackpot. Proof is greater than gold.

They feel like celebrating but instead are quiet, looking through papers and digital pictures.

CUT TO:

INT. WHITE HOUSE, OVAL OFFICE, WASHINGTON DC
- DAY

The meeting is still taking place.

KROELLER (O.S.)
(On speakerphone)
President Abrams, I thought I would bring you
the latest myself.

PRESIDENT
President Kroeller, I am here with Secretary
of State Redstone and Joint Chiefs of Staff
Chairman General Beauchamp and my chief of
Staff, Gene Radamier.

KROELLER (O.S.)
(On speakerphone)
Good morning, gentlemen.

ERNIE
Good morning, sir.

WARREN (OVERLAPPING)
Morning.

GENE
Sir.

                                        CUT TO:

EXT. BANK/EXCHANGE DE SUISSE, ZURICH - DAY

Swiss POLICE take up positions, surrounding
the building.

KROELLER (V.O.)

They have taken over the Bank Exchange. Security officers were released unharmed.

                                    CUT TO:

EXT. BANK/LE MINISTRY DE FINANCE. ZURICH
- DAY

A helicopter hovers overhead while Swiss police surround the building.

KROELLER (V.O.)
Gentlemen, the same situation with the Finance Ministry …

                                    CUT TO:

EXT. BANK/SUISSE D'INTERNATIONAL, SWISS ALPS
- DAY

A helicopter and police flood the area around the building.

KROELLER (V.O.)
And the Bank Suisse D'International.

                                    CUT TO:

INT. WHITE HOUSE, OVAL OFFICE, WASHINGTON DC
- DAY

The emergency meeting continues with the president.

ERNIE
Sir, have you been able to ascertain their resources - (Beat) Men, firepower, communications?

KROELLER (O.S.)
It appears that they are well armed with both
explosives and computers, which is how they
gained access. They apparently have all the
security codes for the doors, vaults, and
security systems.

PRESIDENT
Hostages?

KROELLER (O.S.)
(on speakerphone)
So far, none. None that we know of.

WARREN
What do they want?

KROELLER (O.S.)
(On speakerphone)
They said they will contact us and that if we
try to enter the buildings, they will destroy
them.

ERNIE
President Kroeller, this is General Beauchamp
again. Have you assessed the security of your
backup data and archival systems?

                                          CUT TO:

INT. SKI LODGE, CONFERENCE ROOM, SWISS ALPS
- DAY

On a flat-screen TV monitor connected to a laptop computer, sensitive information is downloaded and the members can barely sit still.
Edna, Peter, Wilson, Alex, Franklin, and Floyd

watch the screen as they hear the voice of Stan's grandson via satellite.

STAN'S GRANDSON (O.S.)
(Via satellite)
Twenty-two, this is sixteen, we are now online via satellite download to Humpty Dumpty database.

They cheer, jumping up and down at what they see.

ALEX
The mother lode

                                    CUT TO:

EXT. EGGHEAD MANSION, SWISS ALPS - DAY

On a large lot, a mansion with a view of homes in a valley sits on a snowy hill.

MALE NARRATOR (V.O.)
Hidden in the Swiss Alps is the Humpty Dumpty headquarters.

INT. MANSION/BASEMENT, CONTROL HEADQUARTERS, SWISS ALPS - DAY

The basement is a high-tech communications center. Cameron, Louis, and Stan's grandson, still clothed in the outfits they wore for the bank heist, cheer alongside seven Men wearing the same attire, with ski masks. We see Edna, Peter, Wilson, Alex, Franklin, and Floyd cheering on a TV monitor.

                                    CUT TO:

INT. WHITE HOUSE, OVAL OFFICE, WASHINGTON DC
- DAY

KROELLER (O.S.)
(on speakerphone)
Gentlemen, I'm afraid they have that, too.

ERNIE
Sir, obviously this is a much larger operation
than we originally thought. We can get assistance from Frankfurt within hours.

KROELLER (O.S.)
(on speakerphone)
General Beauchamp, that won't be necessary. If
needed, we have a 600,000-strong militia that
can be quickly mobilized. Our finance minister
has persuaded me to use that as a last resort.
Thank you, but we believe that is premature.
As soon as we know what they want, I'll contact you, President Abrams.

PRESIDENT
President Kroeller, we'll be here and
available.

KROELLER (O.S.)
(Speakerphone)
I appreciate your readiness. Talk to you later
when we know more. Good-bye.

The president hangs up the phone.

PRESIDENT
(Turns to Ernie)
Ernie, if I should decide to authorize mili-
tary intervention, I will

decide when that should happen. Excuse me; I need to make a call. Don't go far.

                                        CUT TO:

INT. DINING ROOM, ROYAL CARIBBEAN HOTEL, JAMAICA - DAY

Stan and Bertie are nicely dressed, enjoying lunch, when Stan's phone RINGS. Elsie Eubanks, assistant to the president, contacts him. We hear her conversation.

ELSIE (O.S.)
(Stan's phone)
Mr. Watson, Elsie Eubanks. A call from the president, sir.

STAN
(To Bertie)
The president—

                                        CUT TO:

INT. WHITE HOUSE, OVAL OFFICE, WASHINGTON DC - DAY

The president sits at his desk on the phone.

PRESIDENT
(On phone)
Stan, your grandson is being accused of spying for the United States. Intervene and handle this.

                                        CUT TO:

INT. SWISS PRISON, CELLBLOCK, GENEVA - DAY

A PRISON GUARD and a FRENCH ATTORNEY (35, a European, professionally dressed woman) walk past several prison cells until they come to the cell of Stan's grandson, who stands holding the bars.

STAN'S GRANDSON
You're an attorney. Get me out.

The prison guard opens the cell. Stan's grandson exits, walking behind the attorney. The PRISONERS make sexual gestures as they walk by, reaching out toward them.

INT. SWISS PRISON, INTERROGATION ROOM - DAY

The room is bare, with only a large table with a chair and a barred window that has a view of the entrance. The attorney sits and crosses her legs. Stan's grandson paces with anxiety.

FRENCH ATTORNEY
I don't care who you know. You have no options. A homing device tracked you. A geo-positioning satellite system was in your backpack.

STAN'S GRANDSON
I wasn't there! I told you, it's a set-up.

He nervously walks by the window, sees his grandfather, Stan Watson, walking up to the building.

STAN'S GRANDSON (CONT'D)
I don't think there's going to be any more trouble. Looks like someone got the message to the right person.

INT. SWISS PRISON, MAIN OFFICE, GENEVA - DAY

Stan meets with the Swiss AUTHORITIES, who are cordial but antagonistic. As he listens to the evidence, Stan's grandson remains silent but agitated. Then Stan slides a single document across a big conference table.

The Swiss diplomat's jaw drops, and he hastily shows it to some of his cohorts. After a short huddle, the Swiss quickly concede that it's all been a misunderstanding and immediately release the young man. Stan thanks the men and leaves the room. His grandson is exuberant.

STAN
(To grandson)
Make sure your pockets are clean. Return all that's not yours. We don't have dirt in our pockets, only truth.

Stan's grandson nods and hugs his grandfather. They exit the prison, where REPORTERS throng them.

EXT. SWISS PRISON, GENEVA - DAY

Clamoring REPORTERS, taking pictures, asking questions, surround Stan and his grandson. They ignore the reporters. NEWS REPORTER #1 (Asian woman) points her microphone toward Stan.

NEWS REPORTER #1
Mr. Watson, is it true that your grandson was involved in one of the largest heists in U.S. history?

STAN
(To grandson)
Let's get you back to the hotel. Then I have
to get to Washington.

They get into the limousine, and it drives
off.

                                    CUT TO:

EXT. HILTON HOTEL, SWITZERLAND

Busy PEDESTRIAN traffic enters and exits the
hotel. VALETS bring up and park cars.

INT. HILTON HOTEL, PRIVATE SUITE, SWITZERLAND
- DAY

Stan and his grandson stand before the door of
his parents' suite. Stan rings the doorbell.
Stan's SON-IN-LAW (38, African American, light
complexion, light brown eyes) opens the door.

STAN'S SON-IN-LAW
(hugs his son)
Thank God you were released from the hands of
those monsters.
(shakes Stan's hand)
Thank you, my dear friend.

STAN
My son-in-law, it's good to see you again.

STAN'S SON-IN-LAW
We're staying another day to wrap up some
"loose strings," before we head back to the

US. You will meet him at the airport in a couple of days, right?

STAN
We'll be there.
(To Stan's grandson)
Just in case, I've changed your flight to a UPS cargo jet. I want you to be safe. Too much is going on.

                                    CUT TO:

INT. PRESS BRIEFING ROOM, WHITE HOUSE - DAY

President David Abrams is holding a press conference. Stan is by his side.

PRESIDENT
Last question …

A NEWS REPORTER (35, Caucasian man) asks a question, which is indistinct because of the noise and commotion.

PRESIDENT (CONT'D)
Stan's grandson has been released. It was a big misunderstanding. I'll be speaking with President Kroeller in moments. No more questions.

They leave the podium.

PRESIDENT (CONT'D)
(Turns to Stan)
Have you reconsidered running for office?

STAN
It's been considered and denied. Thank you.

CUT TO:

INT. UPS CARGO JET - DAY

We see Stan's grandson sitting in the window seat looking out as the plane starts to
descend.

CUT TO:

INT. AIRPORT, ARRIVALS TERMINAL, WASHINGTON
DC - DAY

Stan, Bertie, Alice, Mattie, and a few FRIENDS
are watching Stan's grandson's plane descend
when it explodes. Everyone screams.

CUT TO:

INT. WHITE HOUSE, CROSS HALL, WASHINGTON DC
- DAY

The president, General Ernie Beauchamp,
Secretary of State Warren Redstone, and Chief
of Staff Gene Radamier are rapidly walking
down Cross Hall when Elsie approaches them.

ELSIE
Mr. President …

PRESIDENT
Yes, Elsie.

ELSIE
Doctor Alex Rutherford from Zurich is on the
line, sir. He's requesting a teleconference

with you and President Kroeller. He knows the reception codes for the cabinet room.

PRESIDENT
A live one, gentleman. Put him through. Let's see who he is and what he wants.

The president and his cabinet turn around and head toward the cabinet room.

INT. WHITE HOUSE, CABINET ROOM, WASHINGTON DC - DAY

The president, Ernie Beauchamp, Warren Redstone, and Gene Radamier enter and take a seat. Alex's face is already on the screen, with Kroeller's face a smaller inset on the larger screen.

ALEX
(On screen)
Good morning, gentlemen. I am Alex Rutherford, head of African
American studies at Harvard. I'll be brief.

The president turns, looks at Ernie, then back toward the screen.

ALEX (CONT'D)
(On screen)
We have seized vital assets and information from the United States and successfully downloaded the information via satellite. We will return the Swiss facilities within Twenty-four hours if you abide by the following conditions.
(beat)
One, we will present and explain our Manifesto

to your representative of our choice. We have selected General Stanley Watson.

ERNIE
(to Alex on screen)
Stan Watson is retired and unavailable. Who else meets your requirements?

ALEX
(on screen)
Send Watson. Have him here within twelve hours. If he isn't, we'll go directly to the press, both in the United States and around the world. Can you imagine what will happen to your bond markets when other countries find out about your inability to honor them?

                                        CUT TO:

INT. PRIVATE JET - NIGHT

Gene is on a flight to Jamaica to meet with Stan Watson. A FLIGHT ATTENDANT (27, Asian woman) offers him a drink.

FLIGHT ATTENDANT
How is your flight to Jamaica, sir?

                                        CUT TO:

INT. ROYAL CARIBBEAN HOTEL, DINING ROOM, JAMAICA - DAY

Stan and Bertie are having breakfast when Gene enters. Stan stands and shakes Gene's hand.

STAN
Gene, we were expecting you.

GENE
Mrs. Watson. I'm very sorry about your grandson. When is the funeral?
(sits down)

STAN
Late this afternoon.

GENE
You know why I'm here. I wouldn't be here, if
there was another way.

STAN
How much time before other options are
exercised?

GENE
It depends on the Swiss and the Humpty Dumpty
Committee. Frankly, we're not sure what we're
dealing with.

STAN
I'm sure that Ernie would prefer that I stay
retired and on vacation, since he is now the
general.

GENE
They want you. Will you do it?

                                        CUT TO:

INT. PRIVATE JET, JAMAICA - DAY

Gene is talking on the phone.

GENE (V.O.)

He was very definite, Mr. President. He refuses to get involved, sir.

                                        CUT TO:

EXT. MANSION, SWISS ALPS - DAY

A light snow comes down on the EGGHEAD secret headquarters.

MALE NARRATOR (V.O.)
Send two men. Intercept Mr. Watson at the funeral. Show him the goods. We'll see who doesn't want to get involved.

                                        CUT TO:

INT. CARIBBEAN HOTEL, WATSON SUITE, JAMAICA - DAY

Stan and Bertie are getting dressed to attend their grandson's funeral.

BERTIE
Stan, this isn't about whether or not duty calls. It's about whether it's okay with me that you jeopardize your life, possibly all our lives. Who knows what these people are capable of?

STAN
This is about defending the country.

BERTIE
No, it's about white men trusting you to do their dirty work, their laundry.

STAN

These are African Americans. Some of whom I
know.

BERTIE
That makes it even worse.

CUT TO:

EXT. CEMETERY, JAMAICA - DAY

It is pouring rain on a gloomy day, as MOURNERS
wearing black attire hold umbrellas. The PASTOR
(54, Caucasian man) says the last words. We
see Stan, Bertie, Alice, Mattie, Stan's son-
in-law, his estranged DAUGHTER, and his grandson's SISTER and BROTHER. FRIENDS and RELATIVES
all grieve.

PASTOR
Know that the Lord, he is God. It is he who
made us, and not we ourselves. We are his people and the sheep of his pasture. Enter into
his gates.

The mourners start to leave.

A black limousine pulls up from a distance.
Two African American MEN wearing long, black
coats exit the vehicle. We recognize one man
as Floyd Davidson, who carries a silver briefcase. The DRIVER is RISHAD ALI (38, African
American man). The men walk toward Stan, who
is huddled with his family.

STAN'S SON-IN-LAW
(to Stan)
I don't want to hear that it's God's will. I
want my son! You made me believe that he was

safe. I believed you. You think that you can
save the world, but you're only man. You can't
save the world, and you didn't save my son!
(falls to knees)
Why, God, did you take my son? Why have you
left me empty?

Stan reaches out to help his son-in-law up,
but the younger man pushes him away. He sobs
with utter brokenness.

Bertie takes hold of Stan. His estranged daughter (37, African American, pretty) acknowl-
edges him, looks at Bertie, and then helps her
husband.

STAN'S DAUGHTER
(to Stan)
Father …

Tears run down Stan's face.

BERTIE
When will she forgive you? You did everything
you could.

STAN
But it wasn't enough.

Alice holds Mattie, who walks behind Stan and
Bertie. Stan wipes his eyes. Floyd and Rishad
approach Stan, pulling him to the side. Bertie
waits with Alice.

FLOYD
(to Stan)
It's important that I tell you our Intentions,
what's at stake, and why we need you.

STAN
The Humpty Dumpty Committee. Okay. Go ahead.

FLOYD
Let's walk …

Stan leaves the men and walks over to Bertie
and Alice.

STAN
(to Bertie)
Honey, there's something I must do. Go to the
reception and carry out your day. I will be in
touch. Say nothing of what you see here. Do
you understand?

BERTIE
Yes. Be careful.

They hug, then Stan joins Floyd and Rishad.
Bertie watches Stan and the men get into the
limousine, then drive off.

INT. LIMOUSINE, CEMETERY, JAMAICA – DAY

Stan is surprised when he sees Alex Rutherford,
one of the heads of the "Egghead Group," in
the limo.

STAN
Alex?

ALEX
Stan, what if I told you that we have conclusive
evidence that Martin Luther King Jr., Malcolm
X, and JFK were killed with the American government's complicity?

STAN
I would say, improbable and shocking. Is it
true that Wilson Powers is with you on this?

ALEX
(dials phone)
Yes, let me put him through to you. He's waiting for our call.

Wilson speaks to them on the speakerphone.

WILSON (O.S.)
Stan, are you there?

STAN
Wilson, what's a Sigma Nu doing holding up a
Swiss Bank?

WILSON (O.S.)
It's been a long time. I'll admit, I should
have called sooner.

STAN
Seriously, Wilson what are you doing mixed up
in all of this?

WILSON (O.S.)
We have, and are still uncovering, some amazing facts. The U.S. Government was involved in
slave trading. Show him …

Alex gives Stan the briefcase. Stan opens it.
It has a laptop computer inside.

Stan boots up and sees, in quick succession,
items listing where billions of dollars in
illicit money came from, and where it went, to

government leaders around the world, past and present. Included in those documents is the black leather bond book.

WILSON (O.S. CONT'D)
We need you, Stan. It's about creating a different future for all African Americans.

Stan holds up the black book.

STAN
What is this?

ALEX
That's an important document. Keep it in a maximum secure place. Never show it to anyone.

WILSON (O.S.)
It's our ace in the hole. I'll tell you about it later.

STAN
Do you know how to get your hands on the money?

CUT TO:

INT. WHITE HOUSE, CABINET ROOM, WASHINGTON DC - NIGHT

The president Gentlemen, the same situation with the Finance Ministry …
meets with Ernie Beauchamp, Warren Redstone, and Gene Radamier. Ernie stands behind a slide projector and shows pictures of the Egghead group. The lights dim.

We see a picture of Alex Rutherford on the screen.

GENE
Alex Stuart Rutherford, 46, PhD from Yale. He arrived at Harvard from Duke in 1991. His notes on the culture wars and his anthology of African American literature are his Best-known works.

Slide changes. We see a picture of Franklin Steadman.

GENE (CONT'D)
Franklin Junius Steadman came to Harvard in 1993 from Princeton. A Philosopher. Key works: *Race Matters*; *Jews and Blacks: A dialogue on race, religion, and culture in America*.

                                        CUT TO:

EXT. AIRPORT RUNWAY, JAMAICA - NIGHT

A limousine pulls up near a private jet. Stan, Alex, Floyd, and Rishad exit the limo and walk hurriedly to the jet.

STAN
What is it that you want?

Peter Straus enters the scene.

ALEX
Stan, this is Peter, George Straus's son.

Stan shakes Peter's hand.

PETER STRAUS

Good evening, sir.

STAN
George Straus from City College?

They enter the jet.

CUT TO:

INT. PRIVATE JET, JAMAICA — NIGHT

Wilson sits comfortably as he waits for Stan to enter.

WILSON
(to Stan)
Yes, George Straus from City College.

STAN
Wilson, there you are.

They shake hands. The hatch closes, and the plane prepares for take-off.

WILSON
Peter has been working on his dissertation over at the University of Geneva. As a historian, he has had complete access to the entire banking and archival system.

STAN
And that's how you found out about the federal slaving?

CUT TO:

INT. UNIVERSITY OF GENEVA, ARCHIVAL ROOM, GENEVA — DAY

Peter Straus pores over stacks of research material. Discovering a cardboard box, he carefully picks it up and reads, "FRAGILE DOCUMENTS."

WILSON (V.O.)
Among other things. Like the fact that the Swiss helped finance Hitler.

Whistling and shaking his head in astonishment, Peter carefully carries each leaf to the copy machine and meticulously copies each page.

PETER STRAUS
Bingo.

CUT TO:

INT. PRIVATE JET, SWITZERLAND – NIGHT

Wilson, Stan, Peter, Floyd, and Alex continue their talk.

STAN
What is it that you expect to achieve with this information, Alex?

ALEX
This is our Manifesto. We want the government to begin doing things that will solve the root problems that are destroying the United States.

WILSON
Stan … runs for office.

CUT TO:

INT. WHITE HOUSE, CABINET ROOM, WASHINGTON DC
- NIGHT

Ernie continues to show slides on the members
of the Eggheads. A picture of Edna Addington
appears on the screen.

ERNIE
Edna Sessions Addington. She came to Harvard
in 1994 from the University of Pennsylvania.
A historian with key works titled: *Righteous
Discontent: The women's movement in the black
Baptist Church.*

The slide changes. A picture of Floyd Davidson
appears on the screen.

ERNIE (CONT'D)
Following Alex from Duke in 1991, was Floyd
Kvamme Davidson. A philosopher, his major
works being: *Color Conscious*, *The Political
Morality of Race,* and *Africa and the Philosophy
of Culture.*

The slide changes. A picture of Wilson Powers
appears on the screen.

ERNIE (CONT'D)
Alex's real coup was attracting Wilson Rustin
Powers from the University of Chicago just
last year. An applied sociologist who had been
recruited with no luck by all the major uni-
versities in the country.
(Beat)
Wilson has been an outspoken critic of all
African American studies programs that do not

measure their success by how they relate their interpretation of scholarship to larger social issues in contemporary life.

The lights turn up.

PRESIDENT
Humpty Dumpty?

WARREN
As in, Eggheads.

GENE
There may not be any pieces all together again.

PRESIDENT
That may be their intention.

ERNIE
These men at his grandson's funeral captured Watson. We have not received word of his whereabouts.

GENE
Mr. President, the other members of the Humpty Dumpty Committee are Cameron Shaherazad, Louis Solomon, and Rishad Ali. All Muslim disciples and lieutenants of Louis Farrakhan. You are all aware of Mr. Farrakhan's point of view, his discussions with Libya, our enemy. His people's participation makes us even more concerned.

                                        CUT TO:

INT. EGGHEAD MANSION, FAMILY ROOM, SWISS ALPS
- NIGHT

In a large room with a wood-burning fireplace, Alex, Wilson, Floyd, Peter, Cameron, Louis, Franklin, and Rishad sit with Stan before a large picture window overlooking a patio with a view of the valley.

Edna enters with glasses of cognac on a silver tray. She gives one to each man as she speaks.

EDNA
Even if the right person were elected, without the right coalitions, no substantive change will occur.

STAN
It works better than force.

EDNA
That's interesting, coming from a former military man.

Edna puts down the tray, and then sits.

STAN
Even the military knows that forceful intervention works only with autocratic rule. Even with autocratic rule in place, it's too expensive to maintain.

ALEX
Hence democracies. We know that. We have something very different in mind.

WILSON
We want those in power to invest differently than in the past.

Tired of the talk, Floyd stands, and walks around room.

FLOYD
To address the problems with action and financing, it will take a shifting of investment from both the government and the major corporations.

STAN
It seems to me that is what the the kings' men and all the kings' horses will be able to put back President is doing now, with his "Initiative of Race."

FLOYD
The dialogue of dishonesty one more time.

EDNA
There has been too much deceit from those who have occupied office.

Wilson stands and walks around the room.

WILSON
Logically, you would think the presidency would be the right place from which to create the needed changes. It's not.

PETER STRAUS
The public has seen too many broken promises. We no longer require that our leaders keep their promises.

Alex stands and walks to the window. He looks outside.

ALEX
It's just another example of a public rela-
tions approach to government that has taken
us further down the path of self-destruction.
(Turns)
Yes, self-destruction.

 (Slams hand on table)
No more advisory boards! No more commissions!
FLOYD

Floyd walks over to the fireplace.

STAN
What do you suggest?

ALEX
First, we and by that I mean all people of
color want a public apology.

STAN
What about the Tuskegee apology?

ALEX
(Chuckles)
The Tuskegee apology? We're sorry for doing
syphilis research on poor black men.

WILSON
As long as they're sorry for syphilis, they
don't have to be sorry for slavery. There have
been other, similar experiments.

FLOYD
They should be sorry. What they did is no different from the Nazis and their treatment of
the Jews.

EDNA
Tuskegee, as tragic as it is, is only a mani-
festation. The
root problem is slavery. We are attempting to
deal with root problems here, in ways that
will bring us back from the brink of self-
annihilation and set a different course that
implements growth.

CUT TO:

INT. ROYAL CARIBBEAN HOTEL, DINING ROOM,
JAMAICA - NIGHT

Bertie sits alone having dinner, as COUPLES
laugh and spoon-feed each other. Somber, she
looks at her watch, then into the fireplace.

CUT TO:

INT. EGGHEAD MANSION, FAMILY ROOM, SWISS ALPS
- NIGHT

The fireplace captures our eyes, as the CAMERA
PULLS BACK we see into Stan's face. He looks
at his watch and mouths, "Bertie." The Egghead
Group sets forth a proposition to Stan to give
to the head of the country.

ALEX
Stan, in addition to an apology, we want slavery reparations for every person of color.
(Beat)
The last piece of our manifesto is the fund-
ing of accessible education, healthcare, and
jobs.

FLOYD
Most important, jobs that are not hazardous to all of our health; jobs in the inner cities that will fund the rebuilding of families again and provide the hope that comes from participation.

STAN
Who is going to pay for all of this?

WILSON
A one-time, 1 percent tax on gross income for the 500 American Corporations and partnerships. The sole proprietor is left alone. That will fund an eight-hundred-billion-dollar hope chest, administered by the Treasury. YES WE DID!!!!

PETER STRAUS
Another related problem, which ties into all of this, is the adversarial nature of conflict. The boundaries between all the groups competing against each other need to disappear.

FLOYD
Private and public distinctions abolished. All entities treated similarly. One political party.

ALEX
No more "us" versus "them."

STAN
It's all us.

WILSON
Exactly.

ALEX
All one …

                                    CUT TO:

EXT. WHITE HOUSE, WASHINGTON DC – MORNING

The sun rises on the White House like a picture postcard.

INT. WHITE HOUSE, OVAL OFFICE, WASHINGTON DC – MORNING

The president meets with Stan, Ernie, Warren, and Gene.

STAN
Well, that's it, sir.

PRESIDENT
(To Ernie)
General, what about the release of the Swiss facilities?

ERNIE
That has already taken place this morning. They are now in Swiss custody.

WARREN
They still have control of our assets, and in effect tie up most of the World Bank funds.

PRESIDENT
Can we have them extradited?

WARREN
I doubt it.

GENE
Has an assessment been made of reconstructing
the computer controls and databases?

ERNIE
COMIREX says, as far as they can determine,
after an initial look-see, they have us, and
everyone else.

                                        CUT TO:

INT. ROYAL CARIBBEAN HOTEL. HALLWAY, JAMAICA
- DAY

A BELLHOP (25, Caucasian man), holds a bouquet
of white lilies in a crystal vase. He rings
the doorbell of the Watson suite. Bertie opens
the door.

BELLHOP
Mrs. Watson?

BERTIE
Yes.

BELLHOP
A delivery from Washington, the kings' men
and all the kings' horses will be able to put
back, and then closes the door.

INT. ROYAL CARIBBEAN HOTEL, WATSON SUITE,
JAMAICA - DAY

Bertie looks at the flowers with loving eyes,
and then reads the card.

STAN (V.O.)

Sweetheart, I'm in Washington and will be home tonight. Love always, Stan.

                                        CUT TO:

INT. WHITE HOUSE, OVAL OFFICE, WASHINGTON DC
- DAY

The president ties up his meeting with Stan, the General, Gene, and Warren.

PRESIDENT
Chevron and AT&T are very pissed off.
(To Stan)
Stan, I want you to get out there and start doing what they want us to do. Maybe we can move this along.

                                        CUT TO:

INT. ROYAL CARIBBEAN HOTEL, WATSON SUITE, JAMAICA - NIGHT

Stan enters, and Bertie greets him with a long hug.

BERTIE
I'm not sure I can be without you anymore.

STAN
I know.
(A steady look)
I think I'm going to run for president. Do you agree I must do this?

Bertie walks into the bedroom, Stan follows.

INT. ROYAL CARIBBEAN HOTEL, WATSON SUITE,
BEDROOM - NIGHT

Stan and Bertie change into their
nightclothes.

BERTIE
Yes, but I'm worried about your safety.

STAN
That's why I have backed away from running for
president—because I didn't want you and the
kids to have to pay the price.

BERTIE
I'm happy to hear that, because—

Bertie draws back the comforter and fluffs the
pillows.

STAN
I also have felt that racial progress was
being made.

BERTIE
As president, you couldn't put all the king's
men and all the king's horses back to influence
it anyway.

STAN
Maybe not …

Bertie gets into bed and Stan follows.

BERTIE
What is the political goal of the first black
president?

STAN
To reverse the effects of slavery.

BERTIE
What is the needed matching commitment of
resources?

STAN
I don't think I'll have any trouble obtaining
the financial commitment to get elected.

BERTIE
Being elected is only a start.

STAN
What, you don't think I can reverse three hun-
dred years of slavery?

BERTIE
Well?

STAN
Bertie, you've always had such confidence in
me.
(Kisses Bertie)
I love you, Bertie.

Bertie turns off the lights.

BERTIE (O.S.)
I love you, too.

                              DISSOLVE TO:

INT. ROYAL CARIBBEAN HOTEL, WATSON SUITE,
BEDROOM - NIGHT

Stan tosses and turns because of an unsettling dream.

DISSOLVE TO:

EXT. CARIBBEAN BEACH, JAMAICA - NIGHT

Stan strolls along the shore, the kings' men and all the kings' horses will be able to put back sees the silhouette of PEOPLE sitting on rocks around a bonfire. One figure gets up and walks toward him. As the man walks toward Stan, his face becomes clearer. It is MARTIN LUTHER KING JR., at the age of his death. King stands before Stan.

KING
Good evening.

STAN
(Puzzled look)
Good evening.

King leads Stan to a circle of people.

KING
Have a seat, General Watson.

STAN
You know me. Has anyone ever told you, you look like Martin Luther King Jr.?

Stan sits on a rock.

KING
Because I am Martin Luther King Jr., Stan. There are some other folks I want you to meet.

THURGOOD MARSHALL, CRAZY HORSE, HARRIET TUBMAN,
MALCOLM X,
W. E. B. DUBOIS, DUKE ELLINGTON, SITTING BULL,
FREDERICK DOUGLASS, and CÉSAR CHAVEZ nod to
Stan when their names are called.

KING (CONT'D)
This is Thurgood Marshall, Crazy Horse,
Harriet Tubman, Malcolm X, W. E. B. Dubois,
Duke Ellington, Sitting Bull, sitting …

Stan chuckles.

KING (CONT'D)
… Frederick Douglass and César Chavez. We know
the struggle you face, Stan.

MALCOLM X
Many of us were faced with the same question.

CRAZY HORSE
The calling of leadership is a gift, a sacred
trust that cannot be refused.

MARSHALL
Many lives have been sacrificed, Stan, so that
you could achieve your successes.

W. E. B. DUBOIS
That brief comfort you will temporarily real-
ize by refusing the presidency is insignifi-
cant compared with the pain and suffering that
will have been endured by your descendants.
Besides, you will always regret not having
fulfilled your capacity.

CÉSAR CHAVEZ

Your family and the children who will follow are your greatest treasure.

KING
You owe it to your descendants and the descendants of all people, whether they are colored or not.

STAN
I wasn't aware that things were so critical right now.

DISSOLVE TO:

INT. ROYAL CARIBBEAN HOTEL, WATSON SUITE, BEDROOM - NIGHT

Stan awakens from his dream and sits up.

STAN
Bertie, I'm running for president.

Bertie turns over.

BERTIE
(Mumbling)
Okay, dear …

CUT TO:

EXT. WATSON HOME, ARLINGTON, the kings' men and all the kings' horses will be able to put back the elegant home, which has a circular driveway.

INT. WATSON HOME, LIVING ROOM, ARLINGTON, VIRGINIA - DAY

Stan and Bertie are being interviewed by
BARBARA WALTERS (early 60s, Caucasian woman,
TV host,) as her CAMERA CREW shoots live from
their living room, which features a baby grand
piano.

BERTIE
(To Walters)
As soon as he announced his candidacy, you can
be certain that someone, somewhere, would see
it as his or her duty and responsibility to
shoot him.

Stan puts his hand on Bertie's to calm her,
knowing she's right.

BERTIE (CONT'D)
This would not only devastate our family, but
the country would be right back where they
were before, maybe worse, with even more hostile feelings about one another.

                                        CUT TO:

EXT. CONFEDERACY BAR, NORTH CAROLINA - DAY

A small bar with a dirt parking lot has motor-
cycles and old, rundown vehicles parked in
its lot. Two Caucasian MEN smoke cigarettes
outside an open door. We hear muttering from
inside.

INT. CONFEDERACY BAR, NORTH CAROLINA - DAY

In this rural bar, motorcyclists and MEN who
look like rednecks fill the bar, drinking and
playing pool, while a few watch the "Barbara
Walters Special" on an overhead TV. RAYMOND

WILLIAMS (32, Caucasian man) mops spilled beer from the bar as MELVIN (36, Caucasian man) and BUCK (42, Caucasian man) watch TV from the bar.

BUCK
(To the TV)
You got that damn straight.

RAYMOND
(Looking at TV)
I don't care if he was in □nam, goddamit! A nigger president? Can you imagine?

                                    CUT TO:

INT. WATSON HOME, LIVING ROOM, ARLINGTON, VIRGINIA - DAY

Barbara Walters interviews the Watson's.

BARBARA WALTERS
Thank you, Mr. and Mrs. Watson. I appreciate your candor. We wish you well in your deliberations about the presidency.
(Beat)
Is it true that you have a three-year-old granddaughter who is talented?

STAN
Yes, it is.

BARBARA WALTERS
We have a special treat for you this evening: Mattie Emory.

Alice, who is sitting at the piano, plays as Mattie sings, standing on the piano bench.

MATTIE
(Sings)
I've thrown away my toys, even my drum and train; I want to make some noise with real live airplanes. Some day I'm going to fly, I'll be a pilot, too, and when I do, how would you like to be my crew?

                                        CUT TO:

INT. CONFEDERACY BAR, NORTH CAROLINA - DAY

The noisy bar has quieted down as Melvin, Buck, and Raymond listen and watch the "Barbara Walters Special" on TV. Mattie's singing fades as bar noises and talking increase.

MATTIE
(Singing on TV)
On the good ship lollipop, it's a sweet trip to the candy shop, there bonbons play on the beach of Peppermint Bay …

MELVIN
(Flying his hand)
She needs one of those little toy airplanes to fly around as she's singing.

RAYMOND
You dumb son of a bitch.

MELVIN
What?

BUCK
Aw, c'mon Raymond, she's just a little girl.

RAYMOND
You dumb sons of bitches.

Raymond storms out. Melvin and Buck shake their heads.

CUT TO:

EXT. STREETS, DOWNTOWN MANHATTAN - DAY

Billboards, posters, and advertising signs saying "STAN WATSON FOR PRESIDENT" are plastered all over the city. Buses display Stan's picture, which has a multicultural picture of the diversity of people at the top, then the words "CRY FREEDOM," then a photograph of Stan standing in front of the American flag, and the words "WE WILL STAND AS ONE."

CUT TO:

EXT. STREETS, DOWNTOWN LOS ANGELES, CALIFORNIA - NIGHT

The same advertising is seen in downtown Los Angeles. There is advertising on buses, and flags of different colors that read, "WE WILL STAND AS ONE," fly around the museum and downtown.

STAN (V.O.)
America, "Cry freedom" from the chains of oppression …

CUT TO:

INT. HOUSE, LIVING ROOM, ALABAMA - NIGHT

A Caucasian FAMILY watches Stan speak on TV. The FATHER 30) and MOTHER (26) sit on the couch and a BOY (6) and GIRL (4) sit on the floor, listening attentively to Stan's speech.

STAN
(On TV)
I will tear down the barriers in our laws. We must break down the barriers in our lives, in our minds, and in our hearts. We will stand as one.

                                        CUT TO:

INT. HOUSE, LIVING ROOM, ARIZONA - NIGHT

A Native American FAMILY, MAN (40), WIFE (35), SON (15), DAUGHTER (12), watches Stan speak on TV.

STAN
(On TV)
I am deeply sorry that my ancestors, some of them called the Buffalo Soldiers, were responsible for advancing across this continent in the name of freedom. In doing so, we pushed Native Americans off their land, often crushing their culture and their livelihood.

The Native American man stands and clenches his fist in agreement. Then his family does the same.

NATIVE AMERICAN MAN
Finally, someone who cares. He sees us, honey. This man has a vision, and we're in it.

                                        CUT TO:

INT. RESTAURANT/BAR, DOWNTOWN LOS ANGELES
- NIGHT

A multicultural group of PEOPLE in a restau-
rant/bar watches Watson's speech on several
flat-screen TVs.

STAN
(On TV)
It is in all Americans' interests that we
treat our old wounds, so that we may build a
new culture that is strengthened by its diversity and shared values.

                                        CUT TO:

INT. APARTMENT, BEDROOM, BROOKLYN, NEW YORK
- NIGHT

An OLD WOMAN (92, African American) watches
Stan's speech sitting up in bed.

STAN
(On TV)
I will direct the introduction of legislation that will pay reparations to all Indian
descendants and descendants of black slaves.

OLD WOMAN
Hallelujah! I wish my great grandmother could
hear you, because she cried freedom.
(Eyes well up)

                                        CUT TO:

INT. HILTON, CAMPAIGN HEADQUARTERS,
ARLINGTON, VIRGINIA - NIGHT

The ballroom, now Stan's headquarters, is where he is giving his speech. REPORTERS and CAMERA CREW flash cameras and film him. Bertie, Alice, and Mattie are seated in the front.

STAN
Though it will not make up for the loss, we will move forward on the recognition that what was done was wrong. In order to survive in the future, we must treat other human beings dif-ferently than before. We need this foundation, not only as Americans, but also for leaders of other nations to follow. Thank you.

A standing ovation.

                                    CUT TO:

EXT. HILTON HOTEL, CAFÉ, PATIO, ARLINGTON, VIRGINIA - DAY

Chief of Staff Gene Radamier has breakfast with Stan and Bertie on the outside patio of the Hilton Hotel.

GENE
(To Bertie)
Well, how's it going?

BERTIE
Fascinating, Gene, it's truly amazing.

GENE
What do you mean?

PATRONS from surrounding tables occasionally look over at Stan. They smile and nod. He replies with a nod.

BERTIE
I did not expect everyone to be so open.

GENE
For instance …

BERTIE
Well, for one thing, the differences between people are very small. We all have the same needs. Everyone wants to be productive and help their families, but there just isn't enough support for those intentions.

Stan's mind is wandering as Gene talks with Bertie.

BERTIE (CONT'D)
Too many barriers have been put in place. If people are excluded in the name of profits, it seems unjustified or just an excuse not to care about people.

GENE
How about you, Stan?

Lost in thought, Stan does not hear Gene because he's thinking about what the Egghead group said.

                                    DISSOLVE TO:

INT. EGGHEAD MANSION, FAMILY ROOM, SWISS ALPS
- NIGHT

In a large room with a wood burning fireplace,
the Egghead group—Alex, Floyd, Edna, Peter,
Wilson, Cameron, Louis, Rishad, and Franklin
sit with Stan before a large picture window.

ALEX
(To Stan)
We want you to go out there and talk to the
people in the inner city, large corporations,
nursing homes, and schools.

WILSON
Just verify what we told you.

FLOYD
We want you to listen as if you were hearing
everything for the first time.

BACK TO:

EXT. CAFÉ, PATIO, ARLINGTON, VIRGINIA – DAY

Gene sees that Stan is lost in thought, so he
calls out again—

GENE
Stan!

STAN
(preoccupied)
Hmm … Oh, the more I find out, the more I
believe that the Humpty Dumpties have accu-
rately assessed our society. We are on the
verge of self-destruction unless we regroup.

BERTIE
That's why we need a different vision, new
leadership, and new hope.

GENE
And Stan, you could be that man. Tonight is
election night.

CUT TO:

EXT. FREETOWN, SIERRA LEONE, WEST AFRICA
- NIGHT

ON SCREEN: FREETOWN WEST AFRICA

The VILLAGERS of Freetown and surrounding cities gather and cheer the news "Stan Watson is elected the new President" as they watch a televised satellite from the Watson headquarters in the United States.

MALE NARRATOR (V.O.)
Ladies and gentlemen, we have a new President tonight. Winning by a Landslide …

CUT TO:

EXT. DOWNTOWN, BRASILIA, BRAZIL - NIGHT

ON SCREEN: BRASILIA BRAZIL

The PEOPLE fill the streets, cheering, waving banners in celebration of the new president-elect. In the heavy city traffic, horns BLOW. They are celebrating in the streets.

MALE NARRATOR (V.O.)
President-elect Watson won the vote of the people, with 349 electoral votes.

EXT. DOWNTOWN OBAMA, JAPAN - DAY

ON SCREEN: JAPAN

PEOPLE in droves are cheering in the streets after seeing on a large outdoor TV screen that

"Stan Watson has won the presidential election
with 349 electoral votes."

MALE NARRATOR (V.O.)
Yes, a new president. The Democrats have control of the House with 242 votes ...

                                        CUT TO:

EXT. CENTRAL PARK, MANHATTAN – NIGHT

ON SCREEN: NEW YORK CITY

Thousands of PEOPLE cheer at one of the Campaign
sites for Stan Watson. On large screens, we
see the results of his win by a landslide. The
response is overwhelming.

MALE NARRATOR (V.O.)
... They needed fifty-one seats to control the
Senate and tonight they have fifty-six votes.
The crowd is roaring. History has been made
tonight. Our first African American president,
Stan Watson.

The crowd goes crazy when Stan, Bertie, Alice,
and Mattie walk onto the platform, waving, in
color-coordinated attire.

MALE NARRATOR (V.O. CONT'D)
And here he is President-elect Stan Watson,
his wife, First Lady Bertie, his daughter
Alice, and granddaughter Mattie. What an amazing night, here in New York City and all over
the United States of America.

                                        CUT TO:

INT. WHITE HOUSE, OVAL OFFICE, WASHINGTON
D.C. - DAY

SLOW PAN to pictures, medals, and swords on
the wall until the CAMERA finds Stan Watson
posing with his new cabinet. We hear MUSIC:
"Hail to the Chief," is playing in the background. We see a photo of Nelson Mandela, Stan
with President Jimmy Carter, Stan in a T-shirt
standing with children in front of a "Boys and
Girls Club," photos of President Reagan and
Clinton, Stan with his command troops from
Vietnam, drawings of the Buffalo Soldiers from
the Civil War, the Medal of Freedom, the Order
of Jamaica, the Eisenhower Leadership Prize
Medal, and a gleaming sword collection from
each branch of the military.

The PRESS takes pictures.

INT. WHITE HOUSE, DIPLOMATIC RECEPTION ROOM
- DAY

Stan enters with SECRET SERVICE MEN, as
his GRANDCHILDREN, Mattie, AMY (8, African
American, long hair, wearing a black and white
dress), STEPHEN (7, African American, light
complexion, green eyes, in suit), WILLIS (9,
African American, wearing suit), and DEXTER
(10, African American, in suit) enter excit-
edly, hugging him.

STAN
(Kneels to Mattie)
My sweet little granddaughter, how I love you
so, and all my grandchildren.

The kids smile.

STAN (CONT'D)
(Picks her up)
Well, Mattie, what do you think of Pa Pa's new digs?

MATTIE
It's so cool.…

STAN
(Hugs her)
Thank you my love!

Stan enters the Cross Hall, nodding to White House STAFF.

INT. WHITE HOUSE, CROSS HALL, WASHINGTON DC - DAY

Stan points to the pictures and the beautiful items in the White House. The kids are polite and well-mannered, in awe at what they see. The Secret Service follows.

AMY
This is beautiful, Pa-Pa. Is this where you work?

WILLIS
Can we see the bowling alley?

DEXTER
And the pool?

Stephen looks at the gear and wire on the Secret Service man.

INT. WHITE HOUSE, KITCHEN, WASHINGTON DC
- DAY

Stan and the kids enter kitchen. The kitchen
STAFF stands.

STAN
(To Staff)
This is my granddaughter Mattie.
She'll be visiting here often.

The kitchen staff nods, with slight smiles.

MATTIE
Pa-Pa I am hungry!

STAN
(Turns to Stephen)
And why are you so quiet?

STEPHEN
I'm just thinking. Maybe one day I will be
president.

The Secret Service men smile.

INT. WHITE HOUSE, OVAL OFFICE, WASHINGTON DC
- DAY

Stan speaks with Chief of Staff Gene
Radamier.

INT. WHITE HOUSE, OFFICE, WASHINGTON DC - DAY

Elsie, the assistant, buzzes the president.

ELSIE
(On phone)

Mr. President, your call from Zurich, sir.

INT. WHITE HOUSE, OVAL OFFICE, WASHINGTON DC
- DAY

Stan and Gene listen on speakerphone.

STAN
Wilson, Alex, how are things going? Gene is
here with me.

CUT TO:

INT. SWISS PRISON, SMALL ROOM, GENEVA - DAY

The Egghead group, Alex, and Wilson speak on
separate phones to Stan at the White House.

ALEX
(On phone)
They could be a whole lot worse …

WILSON
(On phone)
...And a whole lot better, Stan.

ALEX
Being in a jail is still being in jail, even
though it's Swiss.

WILSON
(On phone)
What's going on with the jobs bill for the
inner cities?

                                    CUT TO:

INT. WHITE HOUSE, OVAL OFFICE, WASHINGTON DC
- DAY

Stan and Gene are speaking with Alex and
Wilson.

GENE
We've run into some snags. The gun and tobacco
interests are really flexing their muscles.

                                    CUT TO:

INT. AT&T CORPORATE BUILDING, OFFICE,
WASHINGTON DC - NIGHT

Al Smith (62, Caucasian, man), head of AT&T,
occasionally golfs with the president.

AL
(Speakerphone)
So, what are you staying?

                                    CUT TO:

INT. TELECOMMUNICATIONS BUILDING, SATELLITE
OFFICE – NIGHT

SATELLITE SPECIALIST (38, Caucasian, man)
spies for major corporations.

SATELLITE SPECIALIST
(On phone)
Mr. Smith, it appears the Humpty Dumpties have
figured out a way to change linkups and ID numbers after every call, and then essentially
call-forward the previously used number.

CUT TO:

INT. AT&T CORPORATE BUILDING, OFFICE,
WASHINGTON DC – NIGHT

Al Smith is getting the scoop on the Humpty
Dumpties.

AL
(Speakerphone)
Brilliant! So no call records will leave a
trail. How in the hell are they able to communicate from inside a Swiss jail?

CUT TO:

INT. TELECOMMUNICATIONS BUILDING, SATELLITE
OFFICE – NIGHT

Specialist is still speaking to the head of
AT&T.

SATELLITE SPECIALIST
(On phone)

I have no idea, sir.

                                        CUT TO:

INT. AT&T CORPORATE BUILDING, OFFICE,
WASHINGTON DC - NIGHT

Al Smith finishes his call, as he checks on
Stan.

AL
(Speakerphone)
Stay on it, and report to me directly. Here's
my private pager and satellite number. If you
can't reach me, here are the numbers for John
Wentworth, head of Chevron, and Mark Turner at
Ford. This is a joint project. Only use these
in an emergency.

SATELLITE SPECIALIST (O.S.)
(Speakerphone)
Right.

                                        CUT TO:

EXT. BURNING TREE GOLF CLUB, WASHINGTON DC
- DAY

Stan and Gene play golf with corporate heads Al
Smith and John Wentworth (58, Caucasian man),
head of Chevron, while the Secret Service and
caddies stand by.

STAN
Al Smith, John Wentworth, I need your help
in getting the Inner City Job bill and the
Affirmative Action bill unstuck.

Al and John look at each other, then at Stan. Stan drives a long ball off the tee.

AL
You got it, Stan.

Al drives half the distance.

JOHN
I think the concepts are absolutely sound and necessary, particularly the Affirmative Action legislation. I loved Willis Freeman over at Texaco having to eat crow—Jim Crow, maybe, but still crow.

They laugh. John drives his ball.

AL
Maybe the time just isn't right for the Inner City bill. AT&T will absolutely support you, but a 1 percent hit to gross is going to be hard for many of us to swallow. Don't get me wrong, just that maybe it's time for a redefinition.

They walk along the green.

GENE
By redefinition, do you mean downsizing?

Gene drives his ball.

AL
(Laughing)
Not necessarily. I'm just saying, every now and then most industries go through selective weeding out. The market will decide that there is a new standard.

JOHN
Like telephone telecommunications. In order
for us to evolve from a utility into a worldwide, competitive communications system, we
had to go through a weeding out process.

GENE
Maybe, maybe not. If, before your time, AT&T
had had its way, it would've continued to
enjoy the monopoly it thrived on.

STAN
The real reason we have a worldwide communications system, is due to an
accident of that the defense department acci-
dentally developed a nonproprietary World Wide
Web.

GENE
What I want to know is why redefinition always
has to be at the workers' expense: fewer jobs,
more profits, bigger million-dollar compensation packages for the CEO.
(beat)
Is it true that you have an $8,000-dollar liv-
ing allowance on top of your five-million-dol-
lar salary, and your two-million-dollar stock
options?

JOHN
Gene, focusing on the CEO's compensation
is focusing on the wrong issue. The market
determines that. Why do you think the U.S.
is superior to other countries? Because it
allows businesses to provide the incentives
necessary to reinvest in growth and change.
I really resent your asking Al that question,

particularly since Al is the main reason you are all in office.

AL
Now, come on, John. I'm glad Gene asks these questions. Answers are important. My compensation has nothing to do with my own personal need to subsist. It is all determined by the marketplace.

CUT TO:

INT. TELECOMMUNICATIONS BUILDING, SATELLITE OFFICE - DAY

The satellite specialist who was talking with Al earlier secretly searches the computer room. Occasionally, he looks through the blinds into the other offices, then boots up the computer, which reads, "Top Secret" and asks for a seven-digit ID number. He enters a number, which gives him access.

Al (V.O.)
When I don't compensate my top people, someone else will.

CUT TO:

EXT. BURNING TREE GOLD CLUB, WASHINGTON DC - DAY

Stan, Gene, Al Smith, and John Wentworth are playing golf. Stan drives a long ball off the tee.

AL
And that's how my compensation is determined—by

my Board. It's not a personal issue; it's a
market-driven issue.

GENE
Are your children and their children preoccupied with the worry of how to house, clothe,
and feed themselves and their families?

JOHN
All the king's men and all the king's horses
will be able to!!!
John drives a slice, half the distance of
Stan's drive.

STAN
When limited resources are distributed the
way they are, by the market, over time those
people who do not have influence are driven
into deprivation, hunger, crime, and family
dissolution. They are driven out of having
hope. It is in your best interests to have a
large supply of well-trained people work for
you, is it not?

STAN
In order for them to exist, they need the jobs
that will allow them to raise, feed, and edu-
cate their families.

JOHN
(Looks at Al)
We couldn't agree more.

STAN
Good, then can I rely on your support for the

Inner City Jobs bill and the Affirmative Action
bill.

AL
(Sinking a putt)
Absolutely.

JOHN
Yes, of course. You have always had it.

                                    CUT TO:

INT. WHITE HOUSE, WATSON RESIDENCE, BEDROOM
- NIGHT

Stan and Bertie are comfortably snuggled in
bed.

BERTIE
How does it feel after your first week as
president?

STAN
It wouldn't feel half as good if you weren't
here with me.
(Kisses her)

Bertie smiles, turns over, and then quickly
falls asleep. Stan, dog-tired, looks over at
a stack of papers on his desk, starts to get
out of bed, and then changes his mind. Within
seconds, he's asleep.

Stan is restless, tossing and turning as he
dreams.

                                DISSOLVE TO:

EXT. BEACH, JAMAICA - NIGHT

Stan walks along the beach with his FATHER
(74, African American, slender) toward the
same bonfire as in his previous dream. When
they almost reach the fire, Stan's father stops
walking.

STAN'S FATHER
I cannot go any farther, Stan. I am your father,
and I have introduced you to the best thinkers
in history, heroes.
(Holds Bible to chest)

Stan's father smiles and then fades away like
a cloud. Stan continues to walk until he comes
to a circle of PEOPLE. ABE LINCOLN now sits
with Martin Luther King Jr., THOMAS JEFFERSON,
Crazy Horse, Harriet Tubman, W. E. B. Dubois,
Sitting Bull, César Chavez, and DUKE ELLINGTON
playing keyboard.

STAN
I am not president of the United States. Now
what?

W. E. B. DUBOIS
Stan, a "Talented Tenth" of African Americans
has a great obligation and responsibility to
motivate, lead, and inspire the great underclass to fulfill its potential.

FREDERICK DOUGLASS
You must do the things we wanted to do but
could not.

Martin Luther King Jr. stands, pulls a large,

flaming piece of driftwood from the fire, and gives it to Stan.

KING
The torch has been passed.

BACK TO:

INT. WHITE HOUSE, WATSON RESIDENCE, BEDROOM - NIGHT

Stan tosses and turns in his sleep. Bertie, half-awake, rubs his back, and it settles him.

CUT TO:

EXT. GROCERY STORE, EAST OAKLAND, CALIFORNIA - DAY

Outside a small, local grocery store, STONE PAXTON (13, African American boy), DRUG DEALER, has just made a transaction with a USER when a limousine pulls up. Stone walks up to the vehicle, not noticing that Secret Service vehicles are behind the limo. The window is lowered, revealing …

INT. LIMOUSINE, EAST OAKLAND, CALIFORNIA - DAY

President Stan Watson sits in the limo looking out at Stone.

STONE
You're in luck today, because I have a full range of asilic sebums. You want fast or slow?

STAN
I want to talk to you for a minute. Do you
have time?

STONE
Time is money.

STAN
How are you? I'm Stan Watson, president of the
United States of America. And you are?

STONE
Stone Paxton, because nothing hurts me. Okay,
I'll play your game. What can I do for you,
Mr. President?

Secret Service men approach Stone, protecting
the president. One gives the president a Diet
Pepsi, and he offers it to Stone.

STAN
Would you like one?

STONE
Don't mind if I do.

A HOMELESS MAN and CHILDREN watch from a
distance.

STAN
Do you know what you're doing? Do you know how
smart and intelligent you are? You represent
the hopes and dreams of a whole generation.
You're a businessman, an entrepreneur. You do
marketing, and your own research. How many
people work for you?
You are an employer.

(beat)
Do you know the problem I have with what you're
doing?

STONE
What?

STAN
You're selling the wrong products.

STONE
What other product has these kinds of margins?
A product I don't have to go to school for,
get a degree, pass a test, or get a license to
sell. You see, Mr. President, I can't read.
(Lowers head)

STAN
Stone, I need your help to change all of this,
so that people are safe in their beds at night,
not afraid of being shot by a stray bullet.
(Lifts Stone's head)
Will you help me?

Stan gives Stone a business card. Stone wipes
a tear from his eyes, a slight smile.

STAN (CONT'D)
Call me …

The limo window rolls up, and then the limousine drives off with Stone and PEDESTRIANS
watching. Stone waves.

                                        CUT TO:

EXT. LINCOLN MEMORIAL, WASHINGTON DC - NIGHT

We see Abraham Lincoln and the memorial columns around the rainbow pool.

INT. LINCOLN MEMORIAL, WASHINGTON DC - NIGHT

Stone Paxton stands in front of a mural, admiring it.

MALE NARRATOR (V.O.)
"The decoration above the Gettysburg address in the central group typifies freedom and liberty. The Angel of Truth is giving freedom and Liberty to the slave. The shackles of bondage are falling from the arms and feet. They are guarded by two sibyls."

STONE
Wow. One day my life will count for something.

CUT TO:

INT. EAST MIDDLE SCHOOL, AUDITORIUM, OAKLAND - DAY

In the auditorium, CHILDREN and TEACHERS sit on bleachers waiting for the president to speak. Secret Service is to the right and left of the stage, and they stand at the entrance. Stan talks with Stone Paxton.

STONE
(To President)
Sir, do you mind meeting my friends? They don't believe I know you.

Stan shakes hands with Stone's friends: MC

CRAE, (13, African American boy) and his sister, NISHA (14, African American).

Stan walks out on stage. Stone turns, sticks his tongue out at his friends, and claps quick and hard. The teachers and children stand, cheering. After a few moments, they stop and sit quietly.

STAN
Thank you for having me here today. You're right; you should have the best books and computers to be able to get a good job. I will see that your school is funded adequately so that it will not close.

The teachers and children applaud.

STAN (CONT'D)
You know, I grew up in a neighborhood that was not that different from the one in which you live. The books were old, too. You can get what you want if you are willing to work hard and sacrifice, and not get involved with drugs or anything that will put you in jail. Sometimes the struggle becomes almost impossible, but the main thing is not to give up. I succeeded; so can you.

A standing ovation.

We see Stone Paxton's face. His eyes well up; he is overjoyed, clapping, and then we see Stan's face.

                                              CUT TO:

EXT. WHITE HOUSE, ROSE GARDEN, WASHINGTON DC
- DAY

Bertie is conducting a press conference for
the International Conference on Women's Health
and Human Rights. Mattie is taking pictures
with her disposable camera as she wanders
through the crowd. She runs over to her mother,
Alice.

MATTIE
Mother, can I please see grandpa-pa?

ALICE
Anything, bubby, but hurry back.

MATTIE
Thank you, Ma-ma.
(Runs out)

INT. WHITE HOUSE, OVAL OFFICE, WASHINGTON DC
- DAY

Stan is making the final changes to his State
of the Union speech when Mattie enters, full
of joy.

STAN
Honey, I'm … it's okay, come in. I always have
time for you, little one.

MATTIE
Grandpa-pa, can you take a picture of me sitting at your desk?
(hands him camera)

Mattie gets up on Stan's chair. She sits. Stan
steps back into the center of the room, and

then the glass behind his desk shatters, and Mattie is shot through the back of the chair. She is killed instantly. The bullet is to her head and was aiming for his heart. The alarm SOUNDS. Chaos ensues, with Secret Service men everywhere.

STAN
(screams)
Mattie! Mattie! No!

SOUND becomes indistinct, then muted. We hear MUSIC: "Auld Lang Syne" (the Millennium Mix), and "The Essential," by Kenny G, over the scene (begins 2:50 seconds into song until it ends).

Crying, Stan picks up Mattie. She hangs limp in his arms. Blood is everywhere. Alice and Bertie run in, hysterical.

CUT TO:

EXT. STREET, WASHINGTON DC - DAY

We hear SIRENS as an ambulance and other emergency vehicles rush to the White House. The SOUND becomes indistinct, then muted. We hear MUSIC: "Auld Lang Syne" (the Millennium Mix), and "The Essential," by Kenny G, over the scene.

CUT TO:

INT. RESTAURANT/BAR, DOWNTOWN LOS ANGELES - NIGHT

A multicultural group of PEOPLE in a restaurant/

bar watch a flat-screen TV when breaking news broadcasts. NEWSCASTER #1 (Asian, 37, woman) reports live.

NEWSCASTER #1
(On TV)
Breaking News, there has been an assassination attempt on the
President tonight. Mattie Emory, the president's granddaughter, has been shot and killed.

Shocked faces, gasping and murmuring. SOUND becomes indistinct, then muted. We hear MUSIC: "Auld Lang Syne" (the Millennium Mix), "The Essential" by Kenny G, over the scene.

                                                    CUT TO:

INT. APARTMENT, BEDROOM, BROOKLYN, NEW YORK - NIGHT

The old African American woman is watching TV when her program is interrupted by breaking news on TV. NEWSCASTER #2 (African American, 35, man) reports live.

NEWSCASTER #2
(on TV)
There is very sad news for all of us. Mattie Emory, the President's granddaughter, was brought to Children's Hospital. She was pronounced dead on arrival.

OLD WOMAN (OVERLAPPING)
He kept his promise. He built a memorial for the forgotten people, created jobs, and took

kids off the streets. Now this. Why? They're
the bridge to freedom.

SOUND becomes indistinct, then muted. We hear
MUSIC: "Auld Lang Syne" (the Millennium Mix),
"The Essential" by Kenny G, over the scene.
The old woman weeps.

                                      CUT TO:

EXT. CHILDREN'S HOSPITAL, WASHINGTON DC
- NIGHT

The PRESS flash cameras and interview the
president when he exits the hospital. Stan,
still in bloodied clothing, exits with Alice,
Mattie's mother, and Bertie, who is sobbing
at his side. Secret Service tightly surrounds
them. REPORTERS close in.

REPORTERS
(Clamoring)
Mr. President! Mr. President!

Reporters point their microphones toward the
president.

STAN
(voice cracking)
I will not rest until the cold-blooded killers
have been brought
to justice, whether it's a lone nut or an
international cabal.

NEWS REPORTER #2 trying to break him, pushes
him out of office. You must fight for truth and
righteousness. You are (32, Caucasian man)
approaches Stan.

NEWS REPORTER #2
Mr. President, Mr. President! Do you think
there will be another attempt on your life?

The president looks at him and turns away. The
SOUND becomes indistinct, then muted. We hear
MUSIC: "Auld Lang Syne" (the Millennium Mix),
"The Essential," by Kenny G, over the scene.
Stan and family are escorted into a government
vehicle.

                                        CUT TO:

EXT. POTOMAC PARK, WASHINGTON DC – NIGHT

Hordes of people hold candles and lighters in
remembrance of Mattie. The SOUND is muted. We
hear MUSIC: "Auld Lang Syne" (the Millennium
Mix), "The Essential," by Kenny G, over the
scene.

                                        CUT TO:

EXT. CEMETERY, WASHINGTON DC – DAY

The funeral is closed to the public. However,
throngs of people on the streets watch from
a distance, desiring to attend Mattie Emory's
funeral. We see Stan, Bertie, Alice, his grandchildren, Stan's son-in-law and his estranged
daughter, Gene, David Abrams, Al Smith, John,
Mark, and other familiar faces, as well as the
Secret Service.

We hear MUSIC: "Auld Lang Syne" (the Millennium
Mix), "The Essential," by Kenny G, over the
scene.

CUT TO:

INT. WHITE HOUSE, OVAL OFFICE, WASHINGTON DC
- DAY

Stan sits in his chair looking out the window.
He's drinking Glenlivet, sipping it slowly,
brooding and despondent. He takes a sip, and
then throws the bottle across the room, shat-
tering it on the wall. He stands at the window
and screams outside, slamming his fist into the
wall by the window.

STAN
Shoot now, goddamit! Shoot me, you bastards!
(Tears run down)

The Secret Service agents run in, and then
stop when they see Stan broken with grief.

CUT TO:

EXT. BEACH, WASHINGTON DC - NIGHT

ON SCREEN: SIX MONTHS LATER

The sunset is beautiful. Stan strolls aim-
lessly on the beach, pausing at the remains of
a bonfire.

CUT TO:

INT. TV STUDIO, STUDIO CITY, CALIFORNIA - DAY

On a roundtable political discussion show,
like *This Week with Sam & Cokie,* TV HOST #1
(40, African American woman) and TV HOST #2
(45, Caucasian man), speak on the subject of

the Watson administration in front of a studio AUDIENCE.

TV HOST #1
There's been another Cabinet resignation over a controversy that started after the second honeymoon that resulted from Mattie's death wound down.

TV HOST #2
The buzz around the White House is that President Watson is obsessing over whether the black militant who is the alleged perpetrator is the actual killer.

                                        CUT TO:

INT. WHITE HOUSE, CROSS HALL, WASHINGTON DC
- DAY

Bertie and Gene walk down the hall toward the library.

GENE
Mrs. Watson, there are two more resignations.

BERTIE
Gene, by now don't you think you could call me Bertie? Who is it this time?

INT. WHITE HOUSE, LIBRARY, WASHINGTON DC
- DAY

Bertie and Gene enter the library.

GENE
Ed Brannan.

BERTIE
We could explain away most of the Cabinet member resignations, but to have the vice president resign is hard.

GENE
It gets worse.

INT. WHITE HOUSE, OVAL OFFICE, WASHINGTON DC - DAY

Stan looks out the window and sees DEMONSTRATORS carrying signs that read, "NAACP AND THE BLACK COALITION MARCH" and repeatedly chanting.

GENE (O.S.)
I've been expecting impeachment rumblings, but not from the NAACP.

DEMONSTRATORS
(Chanting)
Stan Watson took our jobs. Stan Watson took our jobs.

When Stan steps back from window, the chanting fades.

Stan
(Signs)
Tobacco money.

DEMONSTRATORS (O.S.)
Stan Watson took our jobs. Stan Watson took our …

INT. WHITE HOUSE, LIBRARY, WASHINGTON DC - DAY

Bertie and Gene are sitting.

GENE
Bertie, you've got to do something. Stan has
lost NAACP AND THE BLACK COALITION MARCH" his
focus. There is a vacuum, and I'm worried
about what is filling it.

BERTIE
I know. Either we do what we came here to do
or we should get out.

INT. WHITE HOUSE, OFFICE, WASHINGTON DC - DAY

Elsie presses the intercom button.

ELSIE
(Into phone)
Mr. President, don't forget your interview
with Oprah, sir. Your
flight is at …

                                        CUT TO:

INT. OPRAH WINFREY SHOW, CHICAGO, ILLINOIS
- DAY

OPRAH WINFREY (50, African American woman),
TV show host, sits before her studio AUDIENCE,
then welcomes her guests.

OPRAH WINFREY
Let's welcome the first African American president of the United States of America and the
first lady.

A standing ovation as Stan and Bertie come out
onto the stage. They shake Oprah's hand, and

then sit. The studio audience continues to clap. Stan, Bertie, and Oprah smile. The clapping finally dissipates.

                                    CUT TO:

INT. HOUSE, LIVING ROOM, ARIZONA - DAY trying to break him, push him out of office. You must fight for truth and righteousness.

The Native American husband and wife watch the Oprah Show. Oprah appears nervous. She turns to Stan and Bertie.

OPRAH WINFREY
(On TV)
Are you sure you want to do this?

STAN
(On TV)
Yes.

OPRAH WINFREY
(On TV)
Welcome to the show, my hidden guests.

Out of the wings comes a beautiful WOMAN (45, Caucasian, brunette), son THOMAS (15, African American-Caucasian mixed, teenager). Oprah, Stan, and Bertie greet them. The studio audience claps until they are seated.

NATIVE AMERICAN MAN
They always try to find dirt, the cutting board of man. Now what?

                                    CUT TO:

INT. OPRAH WINFREY SHOW, CHICAGO, ILLINOIS
- AFTERNOON

Stan reveals his secret.

OPRAH WINFREY
This story was going to be leaked to the press,
so we are airing it first.

STAN
Sometime ago, when Bertie and I were having
trouble in our marriage, I broke my wedding
vow to her.
(with hand gesture)

This is my son Thomas.
(To Thomas)

I'm sorry, son. I never wanted you to be exposed
to the world like this. I have always tried to
protect you.

AN AUDIENCE SPECTATOR (35, Caucasian woman)
stands.

AUDIENCE SPECTATOR #1
You don't represent us. You're nothing but a
common adulterer.

                                        CUT TO:

EXT. STREET, NORTH CAROLINA - NIGHT

On a street in North Carolina, a black limousine
passes a billboard that reads, "IN MISSISSIPPI
I PAY MY BILLS WITH TOBACCO MONEY."

INT. LIMOUSINE, NORTH CAROLINA - NIGHT

Inside the limo, Stan reads the front page of the *New York Times,* which reads, "President Watson's Proposal for Reparations." There is an entourage of Secret Service vehicles traveling behind the limo.

CUT TO:

EXT. CONFEDERACY BAR, NORTH CAROLINA – NIGHT

The limousine and the Secret Service vehicles pull up in front of the bar. We hear SIRENS, and then see flashing lights.

Several police cars enter the scene. The police OFFICERS exit their vehicles and surround the building.

INT. CONFEDERACY BAR, NORTH CAROLINA – NIGHT

The PEOPLE in the bar look outside and scramble for the exits, ditching their drugs and illegal weapons as they go, but nobody can leave. Then Raymond sees that it's the president's car.

RAYMOND
He's here for me. I sent the president an e-mail and told him that I wasn't going to pay a damn dime for any memorial or anything else.

MELVIN
Raymond … you threatened him.

RAYMOND
No, I didn't. I just told him …

BUCK
You're a dead man. That was a threat.

RAYMOND
I told him if he didn't like it he could come
down and we could fight it out to see who is
right.

BUCK
They're going to lock you up.

RAYMOND
Shut up, Buck! You don't know what you're
talking—

Melvin looks out the window.

MELVIN
Here he comes, prizefighter. I tell you, you're
toast, because he's mad.

Some of Raymond's other friends are impressed,
as they mumble. Stan storms in with Secret
Service all around.

STAN
Who is Raymond?

No one answers.

STAN (CONT'D)
I said, "Who is—

MELVIN
(Pointing)
He is. He's Raymond.

Stan walks up to Raymond.

STAN
Are you Raymond?

RAYMOND
I am.
(Flippant)
Did you get my e-mail?

Stan grabs him by the shirt collar and raises
his fist.

STAN
What did you call me? Nigger!

Stan punches Raymond in the face, and Raymond
falls to the floor. Stan picks him up and beats
the living tar out of him. We see that something is very wrong with Stan.

BUCK
He's killing him!

Raymond's friends hold back another friend
who wants to jump in and save him. Stan is
unleashing bottled anger and if the Secret
Service doesn't stop him, he will kill this
man. Two Secret Service men pull Stan off
Raymond. Secret Service Agent #1 (45, African
American, bald) speaks to Stan.

SECRET SERVICE AGENT #1
(Holding Stan)
Sir, please. Enough.

Stan calms. The local police run in with guns

drawn toward Raymond. He is a bloodied mess lying on the floor.

RAYMOND
(To police)
Nothing's wrong here … but me.

The police turn to exit when Raymond's leg begins to shake violently, and he breaks down into hysterics.

RAYMOND (CONT'D)
(Weeping)
How do I get it out? How do I get out the hate that my father fed me, the beatings, and the rapes?

He remembers the past, the pain, and the torment of what he saw and now lives with.

DISSOLVE TO:

EXT. VACANT FIELD, NORTH CAROLINA – NIGHT
(FLASHBACK)

A group of KU KLUX KLAN MEMBERS in white hooded apparel burn a BLACK MAN on a cross as a small CHILD wearing a KKK outfit watches. The man on the cross screams.

RAYMOND (V.O.)
How do I get it out? The hatred in my heart. He whipped me if I talked to the Jews. He tied me up if I talked with the Blacks. He said, "Burn them."

DISSOLVE TO:

INT. CONFEDERACY BAR, NORTH CAROLINA – NIGHT

Raymond relieves his torment, as everyone watches.

RAYMOND
He said that we were better, but we're nothing but poor white trash. How do I get out what's eating me inside, Stan? Help me.

MELVIN
Damn.

Everyone is shocked. Stan walks up to Raymond, extends his right hand, and helps him up. Raymond clutches him like a small child freed from falling into a well.

STAN
Raymond, you get it out with love.

CUT TO:

INT. HOTEL, PRESIDENTIAL SUITE, RALEIGH NORTH CAROLINA. – NIGHT

Stan and Bertie are watching the evening news when they see "Breaking News." Stan's face is plastered across the TV screen.

We hear NEWSCASTER #3 (35, Caucasian man), President in trouble! Stan pours two drinks and hands one to Bertie.

NEWSCASTER #3
(On TV)
Breaking news. Tonight in the Confederacy Bar in Raleigh, North Carolina, a fight broke out.

The president and Secret Service were seen leaving the bar. It appears that President Watson may have been …

BERTIE (OVERLAPPING)
Sometimes you do damn foolish things.

Bertie turns off the TV.

STAN
But honey, this was between love and hate …
and love won. A man was freed tonight.

They lift their drinks and toast.

STAN (CONT'D)
You know, you were right from the beginning.

BERTIE
About what?

STAN
About having the goal match the commitment. I
should never have done this to us.

BERTIE
This is a wake-up call. We are in a war. Just
because they caught the sniper doesn't change
anything.

                                        CUT TO:

EXT. BRICK HOUSE, WASHINGTON DC - NIGHT

A SWAT team surrounds the house, breaks down
the front door, and enters.

BERTIE (V.O.)
The difference now is that we are all on the
battlefield.

INT. BRICK HOUSE, BASEMENT, WASHINGTON DC
- NIGHT

The SWAT team searches the rooms, and then breaks down the basement door, where they see pictures of the president's family on the wall, pictures of where they have gone, and markings showing where and how the president would be killed. Weapons are confiscated.

Beneath a hidden door in the floor, the finds and handcuffs the sniper (45, Caucasian man), leading him upstairs and out of the house.

                                    DISSOLVE TO:

INT. HOTEL, PRESIDENTIAL SUITE, RALEIGH,
NORTH CAROLINA - NIGHT

Bertie tells Stan how she really feels.

BERTIE
Before, you were there without us, physically. It was difficult, living in most of the places we had to, raising the children especially in the early years. We gave up a lot for you to do what you did for a living, not knowing if you would be killed.

STAN
Bertie …

BERTIE
The stress was sometimes unbearable. I, in many ways, would rather have been in the battle.

STAN
No, you wouldn't.

BERTIE
How do you know what I wanted? Did you ever ask?

STAN
No. I'm sorry, Bertie. I'd give anything to have her back.

BERTIE
Was justice ever achieved for the families of Martin Luther King Jr., John Kennedy, and Malcolm X? This is a war. Was slavery about race? Slavery was about economics. Color and race has been a handy label, a disguise. What's the one truth about war that you came away from Vietnam with?

STAN
In order to be successful, you need a clear political objective and matching resource commitment.

BERTIE
So what is this war about?

STAN
Economics?

BERTIE
What is your objective in the war we are now in?

STAN
To isolate the enemy from his economic resources, I need to obtain the necessary resource commitment that matches that objective.

BERTIE
(Salutes)
You may go to the head of the class, soldier.
Carry on, and not as you were.

                              CUT TO:

EXT. WHITE HOUSE, WASHINGTON DC - DAY

View of the White House.

EXT. WHITE HOUSE, WATSON RESIDENCE, TERRACE
- DAY

GEORGE, the butler (60, Caucasian man) serves
Stan and Bertie breakfast.

BERTIE
Thank you, George.

George nods, then exits.

BERTIE (CONT'D)
(To Stan)
Have you thought about filling the vice
presidency?

STAN
Yes.

BERTIE
Good.

STAN
I want Dave Abrams to take it.

BERTIE
Not after all those terrible things he said

about you during the campaign! How could you trust him? He's a politician, Stan.

STAN
If he believed those things, if not, I believe he will enhance and advance my plan.

BERTIE
What does Gene think?

STAN
I wanted to talk to you first.

BERTIE
Why do you want him?

STAN
He has an established network for enacting legislation. I need to be out there influencing people who will influence the future children. They are our real hope.

BERTIE
It sounds good. I just hope they don't do too much damage back here in Washington.

STAN
We will begin to build a true coalition government.

BERTIE
It's good to have you back.

She affectionately kisses him.

                                        CUT TO:

INT. WHITE HOUSE, OVAL OFFICE, WASHINGTON DC
- DAY

Stan speaks to members of the Egghead Group.

STAN
(Speakerphone)
Wilson, Alex, you like the plan?

                                    CUT TO:

INT. SWISS PRISON, SMALL ROOM, GENEVA - DAY

From an isolated place within the prison, Alex
Rutherford and Wilson Powers secretly talk to
the president.

ALEX
(On phone)
Only if you have something on Dave that he
needs or wants. You can't trust him to carry
out our programs.

WILSON
(On phone)
I like you getting out into the schools. Don't
go below the second grade or above the eighth.
By middle school, they're already caught up.

ALEX
(On phone)
In order for any of this to work, there have
to be jobs, good jobs, at the end of the
pipeline.

                                    CUT TO:

INT. WHITE HOUSE, OVAL OFFICE, WASHINGTON DC
- DAY

Stan is still speaking with Alex and Wilson,
who are in prison.

STAN
That's why I need David. I can't get Affirmative
Action and the Inner City Jobs bills in place
in the time I have.

ALEX (O.S.)
(On speakerphone)
Maybe you need to stay longer. It's a good
plan. Good luck, Mr. President.

Stan hangs up, and then is buzzed by Elsie,
his assistant.

ELSIE (O.S.)
Mr. President, Mr. David Abrams and Mr. Gene
Radamier are here.

STAN
Send them in. Thank you, Elsie.

David and Gene enter.

STAN (CONT'D)
David, Gene. Thanks for coming on such short
notice.

GENE
(Nods)
Mr. President—

They have a seat.

DAVID
How's it going, Mr. President? I was surprised
to hear from you.

STAN
David, I need a vice president who will be
responsible for the Affirmative Action and
Inner City Jobs bills being passed. Will you
take the job?

DAVID
Good God, Stan. Mr. President. You've got to
be out of your mind, with all due respect.

STAN
No, hear me out. The presidency is institu-
tionally flawed. It's not designed to create
the kind of change that is needed now. The
successful candidate is chosen for his ability to speak a philosophy. Not for his ability
to get legislation enacted through Congress.
The problem is that effective coalitions have
to be built with the opposition. I need you,
David. Will you do it?

DAVID
Potentially, you have another term after this
one.

STAN
Let's say I don't run for re-election. Does
that make it worth your while?

DAVID
If I have your agreement to support my return
as president.

STAN

You do. Assuming you get this legislation passed.

GENE
(To Stan)
If you were a target before, with David the heir apparent, you will become even more of a target.

STAN
Not if we announce that I will not run for re-election right now and that Dave is the man. If I'm a lame duck, I may be taken out of the crosshairs.

GENE
Is that why you're doing this?

STAN
I'm doing it because it's best for the country. Right here, in the nation's capital, there are schools that are 100 percent minority. African Americans economically segregated. Youngsters who've never come across the Anacostia River to visit the Washington Monument. There are condominiums in New York where the president's son-in-law can't own a home. Not because he doesn't have the money or the credit or the references, but because of the color of his skin. Zip codes 10021 and 10022 in the largest city in the United States. Not in a small southern town, but in New York City.

DAVID
If I'm doing all the work, what will you be doing during the remainder of this term?

STAN

(Stands)
Going back to school.

                                    CUT TO:

INT. WHITE HOUSE, WATSON RESIDENCE, LIVING
ROOM - DAY

Bertie sips coffee as she watches the Oprah
Winfrey Show.

OPRAH WINFREY
(On TV)
So, what do you all think about that? We finally
get an African
American president, and he quits halfway
through his term.

Bertie lowers her cup.

BERTIE
Hey, you're supposed to be on our side.

An AUDIENCE MEMBER (35, African American woman)
shouts.

AUDIENCE MEMBER #2
(On TV)
I think they got to him. Just like we all got
hoodwinked!!

BERTIE
Then you don't know my Stan.

Another AUDIENCE MEMBER (40, Caucasian woman)
stands.

AUDIENCE MEMBER #3

(On TV)
Yes, when his granddaughter was killed.

BERTIE
You better shut up and sit down, before…… I
am sorry.

The audience member sits.

                                    CUT TO:

INT. LINCOLN ELEMENTARY, OAKLAND, CALIFORNIA
- DAY

Stan sits among a class of thirty minority
CHILDREN in the third grade, with the desks
arranged in a circle. He laughs, and then the
children do. Their TEACHER stands in the back
along with Secret Service.

INT. LINCOLN ELEMENTARY, HALLWAY, OAKLAND
- DAY

Two older African American BOYS and a Hispanic
BOY are beating up a third grader, ANTHONY
HIGGENBOTHAM (9, African American boy, boys
run away with the third-grader's lunch.

STAN
Hey, come back here.
(To Secret Service)
Get them …

The Secret Service catch HERSHELL WALLACE,
OAKLAND, CALIFORNIA - DAY

Hershell and Anthony sit on jump seats, fac-
ing Stan.

STAN
So that's my plan. Are you willing to work
with me?

HERSHELL
Uh huh.

STAN
No. I want you to respond by saying, "Yes, sir
or no, sir."

HERSHELL
Yes, sir.

STAN
Okay … and Anthony, I want you to be early to
all of your classes. Not just on time, but
early. Okay?

ANTHONY
Yes, sir.

STAN
I want both of you to come up with a plan to
make this school better
and report to me next week. This plan will represent not just your own thoughts, but those
of the other students and your friends. Most
important, your report will represent just the
things on which you two agree. I do not want
to hear about the things you disagree on. Is
that understood?

ANTHONY
You mean safer.

STAN

If that's what you think is needed.

HERSHELL
You mean like the lunches?

STAN
That's right. Anything that you think will
make it possible for you to get the best education not just a good one; the best one.
Understood?

HERSHELL/ANTHONY
Yes, sir.

STAN
(Shaking hands)
Hershell, Anthony. It's a real honor to be
working with you.

Stan opens the door and they climb out in
awe.

STAN
Bye …

HERSHELL
Bye … see you next week.

ANTHONY
Bye, sir.

                                    CUT TO:

EXT. BURNING TREE GOLF CLUB, WASHINGTON DC
- DAY

John Wentworth, head of Chevron, and the new
vice president, David Abrams, finish putting

the eighteenth green and add up their scores.
John laughs and hands David some money.

EXT. BURNING TREE GOLF CLUB, TERRACE,
WASHINGTON - DAY

Al Smith, head of AT&T, and John are having
cocktails when Mark and David enter, joining
them.

JOHN
(To David)
Mr. President—I mean Vice President—you are
in rare form. Much more competitive now that
you're back.

DAVID
I've had time to practice.

AL
We're glad to see you back, David.
How are thinks going on the hill.

DAVID
Pretty well. We should be within a couple
of weeks of a vote in the Senate and probably sooner in the House on the Jobs Bill.
Affirmative Action is a little slower.

AL
Is capital gains recension lined up?

DAVID
I see no problems.

MARK
How about estate inheritance?

DAVID
Looks good.

JOHN
Everything is great, but we still don't have
our assets unfrozen.

DAVID
I'm working on that, too.

AL
We'll force him out, weaken him. We need you
to deliver on this, Dave.

DAVID
Understood.

CUT TO:

INT. LIMOUSINE, OAKLAND, CALIFORNIA - DAY

The president's limo slows when he sees Stone
Paxton walking down a neighborhood street.
Stan taps on the divider window.

STAN
(To DRIVER)
Pull over.

The limousine pulls over and stops. The window
lowers and Stone Paxton walks up, smiling.

STONE
(To Stan)
I was sorry to hear 'bout your granddaughter.
That must've been hard to take, even living in
the White House. Did they get who did it?

STAN
Yes, but that bullet was really meant for me.

                                    CUT TO:

EXT. GENE'S CAR, WASHINGTON BRIDGE,
WASHINGTON - NIGHT

Gene is being chased by a black car with
tinted windows. He dodges the vehicle several
times when another car hits it, freeing him.
SPECTATORS drive slowly due to the car nearly
hanging off the bridge. We hear SIRENS, and
then see POLICE.

                                    CUT TO:

INT. WHITE HOUSE, VICE PRESIDENT'S OFFICE,
WASHINGTON - DAY

The vice president discusses some things with
Gene.

DAVID
We've had some defection on the jobs bill. We
need to play our capital gains card.

GENE
Oh, c'mon, David. They always do this.

DAVID
This is different. The dynamics are very dif-
ferent. You know that I want this as much as
Stan does.

GENE
(Suspicious look)
We can't cave in. It's the centerpiece to the

whole enactment. Besides, the budget deficit limits have kicked in, and we really don't have the kind of latitude we had when you were in office.

DAVID
Gene, in case you haven't noticed, I am in office now. Incidentally, Gene, I need you to find out whether or not Stan is in direct contact with those Humpty Dumpty people. Can you do that?

GENE
(Getting up)
I'll see what I can do.

Gene starts to walk away.

DAVID
Oh … and Gene—
(Gene turns)
I need the link numbers on their communication frequencies.

GENE
Assuming there is direct contact, right.

INT. WHITE HOUSE, OFFICE, WASHINGTON DC - DAY

Elsie looks through a file drawer.

ELSIE
Where is my call log? Ah, there you are. I've been looking all over for you.

Then she makes a call as she looks through it.

ELSIE (CONT'D)
(On phone)
Oh, hi, Carolyn, this is Elsie over at the White House. No. The vice president wanted me to get back to him with some information. The number he was looking for is 1-700-

CUT TO:

INT. ELEMENTARY SCHOOL, COMPUTER LAB, OAKLAND - DAY

Anthony, Hershell, and other CHILDREN are jumping up and down when they see their new computer lab, tied with red ribbons. Then Stan enters, and they clap with joy, running up to him.

ANTHONY
(To Stan)
Thank you, sir, for the computers, they're beautiful.

HERSHELL
That's what we needed: mentors and computers, and you're our mentor.

CUT TO:

INT. WHITE HOUSE, Are you sure you want to put the rest of your family in jeopardy like this?
WASHINGTON DC - DAY

Stan meets with David and Gene.

STAN
What we need are tax incentives:

childcare, education incentives for both parents and charter schools, tax credits for mentoring, internships and on premise healthcare with nutrition.

DAVID
Whatever you want, but it will cost you.

STAN
Vice president, can you roll it all into one bill?

DAVID
Possibly.

GENE
You have an ace in the hole if you want to play it.

DAVID
What's that?

GENE
The tobacco suit: $368.5 billion. And if that settles, all the healthcare and class action suits that are lining up will be blocked.

DAVID
We probably ought to save that one.

GENE
The window is now.

STAN
I agree. Are you sure you want to put the rest of your family in jeopardy like this?

DAVID
(Angry)
Gentlemen, I'm not saying you're wrong, but
maybe we need to keep some of our powder dry.

                                    CUT TO:

EXT. POTOMAC PARK, WASHINGTON DC - NIGHT

Overlooking the park, a police cruiser
approaches a parked car. The OFFICER (32,
Hispanic man) looks and sees a MAN asleep.
When he approaches the vehicle, he sees that
the man, Chief of Staff Gene Radamier, is shot
in the head, dead.

                                    CUT TO:

INT. HOUSE, BATHROOM, ARLINGTON, VIRGINIA
- DAY

A WOMAN hums to music on the radio as she takes
a shower until she hears tragic news from the
RADIO HOST.

RADIO VOICE
(On radio)
Chief of Staff Gene Radamier was found dead
late last night. He was shot and killed at
Potomac Park, where police found his body.
Radamier was recently divorced, and this is
being considered a possible suicide, but an
investigation is …

                                    CUT TO:

INT. WHITE HOUSE, OVAL OFFICE, WASHINGTON DC
- DAY

Stan meets with the vice president.

DAVID
It's a loss to us all. Gene and I were together
for many years. I valued him a great deal.
Susan and the kids must be devastated.

STAN
Yes. Bertie is over there now.

DAVID
Stan, I need to talk to you about the Affirmative
Action and the Jobs/Education bill.

STAN
Can't it wait?

DAVID
No, it can't, Mr. President. We need you to
sign the bill as it now stands. This pro-
vides for all of the incentives you wanted
and in return settles the Tobacco Settlement
Agreement.

STAN
What about capital gains?

DAVID
We need 80 percent protection.

STAN
We? David, you know what that will do. The
highest I will go is 30 percent.

DAVID
Stan, there is no good time for what I have to
tell you.

(Beat)
You do not have a choice.

STAN
Bullshit. I can veto it.

DAVID
No, you can't. If you do, you will place your
entire family at risk.

STAN
What do you mean?

DAVID
It's true that the bullet that killed Mattie
was meant for you,
but we need you, so unless you sign this bill
as it stands, you put Bertie, and the rest of
your family at risk.

STAN
Put them at risk with whom?

DAVID
Whom do you think, Stan? It's not an individ-
ual, per se; it's the corporate infrastructure
that pays for all of this.

STAN
Get out!

DAVID
And by the way, Stan, I want to be involved
with all conversations you may have with the
Humpty Dumpties.

STAN

I want your resignation on my desk by the end
of the day.

DAVID
That's not going to happen, Stan.

Stan gets up, and David reaches for the door.

DAVID (CONT'D)
The bill should be ready for your signature in
about thirty days.

David leaves. Stan turns, walks to the window,
and looks out. Then he walks to his desk and
presses the intercom button.

STAN
(Into intercom)
Elsie, bring your call log printout and come
in here, please.

ELSIE (O.S.)
Yes, sir.

Stan sits. Elsie enters and closes the door
behind her.

STAN
Let me see the last few days of calls.

ELSIE
Here they are, back three weeks.

STAN
What's this one?

ELSIE
Oh, that's the satellite call to Switzerland.

A conference call with Mr. Powers and Rutherford.

STAN
Has anyone asked for this number?

ELSIE
Only the vice president.

STAN (CONT'D)
I need a computer set up here with modem capa-
bility. I want to be
able to communicate with the kids at Lincoln
Elementary and East
] School.

Elsie starts to leave.

STAN (CONT'D)
And Elsie,
(She turns)
Make sure it's secured.

Elsie nods, then exits.

                                              CUT TO:

EXT. CEMETERY, ARLINGTON, VIRGINIA - DAY

At Gene Radamier's funeral, Stan and Bertie
sit next to Gene's ex-wife, SUSAN RADAMIER
(40, Caucasian), son MIKIE (15, Caucasian),
son KEN (20, Caucasian) and daughter KAREN
(17, Caucasian). The PRIEST (54, Caucasian)
says the last words before the coffin. Then
Susan stands, tosses a flower onto many flowers
on the coffin and pulls Bertie to the side.

SUSAN RADAMIER
(Whispers)
Gene didn't kill himself, Bertie. He was
murdered.

Stan watches David when he looks at the coffin, then back at him and Bertie, because
David is thinking, "You're next."

CUT TO:

INT. LINCOLN ELEMENTARY, COMPUTER LAB,
OAKLAND, CALIFORNIA - DAY

Stan, Secret Service, Hershell, Anthony, and
the PRINCIPAL (27, Caucasian woman) are shocked
when they see all the equipment trashed. On
the walls are spray-painted messages: "Impede,
Shackles, Fetters, Manacles," and "The Chains
of Oppression will remain."

PRINCIPAL
Just when we were making progress, something
like this happens.
From the spray paint, it appears that a local
gang did it.

HERSHELL
The Nobles didn't do it.

PRINCIPAL
How can you be sure?

HERSHELL
I used to belong.

ANTHONY
(Reads)

"The chains of oppression will remain." What does it mean?

STAN
It's a message from the enemy.

CUT TO:

INT. LIMOUSINE, OAKLAND, CALIFORNIA - DAY

Anthony insists on speaking to the president alone.

ANTHONY
Mr. President, I received a phone call last night from Wilson Powers. He said he couldn't contact you directly anymore, and to tell you that John, Al, and Mark are the "we." He also said to tell you that you must move very quickly.

STAN
Okay, Anthony, that's what I needed to know. You and Hershell better lie low. I wouldn't be surprised if the lab at East Middle School has been trashed, too.

CUT TO:

INT. EAST MIDDLE SCHOOL, COMPUTER LAB, OAKLAND, CALIFORNIA - DAY

Stone's friends, Nisha, Mc Crae, and ANITA (13, Hispanic) stand with their TEACHER and other STUDENTS in shock. The computer lab has the same spray-painted messages and damage.

MC CRAE

Shit. How are we gonna get back to the Prez?

                                        CUT TO:

INT. WHITE HOUSE, OVAL OFFICE, WASHINGTON DC
- DAY

Stan is sitting at his laptop when a message
pops up.

MC CRAE (O.S.)
(on computer screen)
Prez. This is Mc Crae. Are you there?

STAN (V.O.)
(Types into computer)
Yes, I'm here. I've been worried about you,
Anita, and Nisha.

MC CRAE (O.S.)
(On computer screen)
We're fine. We had to move operations.

STAN (V.O.)
(Types into computer)
Was your computer lab vandalized?

MC CRAE (O.S.)
(On computer screen)
Yes.

STAN (V.O.)
(Types on computer)
They weren't vandals. You may be in danger, so
be careful. We're
going ahead with Operation Easter as soon as
I can set it up, so
heads up.

CUT TO:

EXT. BURNING TREE GOLF CLUB. WASHINGTON D.C.
- AFTERNOON

Stan, Al, John, and Mark are at the first tee.
A Secret Service drives the presidential golf
cart and the other serves as caddy. Three
other caddies stand at a distance.

JOHN
Shall we make it interesting?

AL
I'm game. How about you Stan?

STAN
How 'bout $10,000 a hole, with a kicker at
the end of an additional $20,000 for the best
score?

AL
Scratch.

STAN
Why not?

JOHN
Sounds good to me.

MARK
With bets like these, you must be on your fifth
printing with that book of yours, or you've
been practicing.

STAN
Not necessarily. You guys just don't have a
chance.

Stan tees off, nailing a lofty 350-yard drive.

AL
Not bad, Mr. President.

Al tees off with a high 250-yard shot.

JOHN
You people aren't fooling around today, are you?

John drives the ball a long, low line drive 250 yards.

MARK
How's the vote going on the Tax/Jobs bill?

Mark drives a line drive 260 yards.

STAN
It just passed the House. Just so you all know, as it stands, I will veto it, so you better not let it get through the House.

AL
Mr. President, have you talked to David about this?

STAN
Al, I thought I'd go right to the top instead.

JOHN
You give us way too much credit.

STAN

John, cut the crap. I won't let you run this country anymore.

AL
You don't have a choice, Stan.

MARK
C'mon, you guys, lighten up, it's a beautiful day.

STAN
Not for thirty million African Americans and a growing number of
economically excluded other Americans, Mark.

EXT. BURNING TREE GOLF CLUB, NINTH GREEN - DAY

Stan sinks a short putt. Al misses his putt and must make two putts. Mark and John three putts each.

AL
So, where do we stand on the front nine?

STAN
Al, you owe me 30k, Mark, 40, and John, you owe me 60.

AL
Double or nothing for the back nine. Agreed?

Stan, Mark, and John nod.

EXT. BURNING TREE GOLF CLUB, EIGHTEENTH GREEN - DAY

Al one putts, Mark three putts, John two putts, and Stan sinks a twenty-five-foot beauty.

EXT. BURNING TREE GOLF CLUB, TERRACE – DAY

The WAITRESS (28, Caucasian, blonde) enters to take their order.

WAITRESS
What can I serve you, gentlemen?

STAN
Cuba Libra with Jamaican rum.

MARK
Glenfiddich with a splash.

AL
Red Hook.

JOHN
Dewar's with a splash.

The waitress exits.

AL
(to Stan)
What's the damage?

STAN
Here's what you need to do, gentlemen. Have the Tax/Job bill
amended to include the package of incentives I originally proposed: capital gains protection not to exceed 30 percent. Have the Affirmative Action bill passed in both houses, and have those bills on my desk in a week or you can kiss your assets good-bye.

CUT TO:

EXT. WATSON HOME, ARLINGTON, VIRGINIA - DAY

Dressed as FBI agents, RODNEY (34, Caucasian, dark hair), and WILBUR (36, Caucasian, dirty blond) walk up to the front door. They look through the windows and, seeing no one, they disarm the electronic security system and enter.

INT. NEIGHBOR'S HOME, ARLINGTON, VIRGINIA - DAY

The NEIGHBOR (75, Caucasian woman), drawn to the window by a noise, sees two men enter Stan's house.

NEIGHBOR
(dials police)
That's the president's house.

INT. WATSON HOME, LIVING ROOM, ARLINGTON, VIRGINIA - DAY

We see pictures of Mattie and the Watson family on the piano and on the walls. Rodney and Wilbur split up. Rodney enters the kitchen, and Wilbur goes upstairs.

CUT TO:

EXT. BURNING TREE GOLF CLUB, TERRACE - DAY

Stan, Mark, Al, and John continue their meeting over drinks.

AL
You played a helluva game, Mr. President, but all told, we can't
owe you much more than $30,000, for which I'm sure you will accept our checks.

STAN
Your checks are no good. And this isn't about golf today. It's about these bills in Congress. It's about returning this country to those for whom it was intended.

JOHN
What do you mean our checks are no good?

STAN
I have seized control of all of your accounts. They no longer exist. I have also taken your trust funds, stock option accounts, and even the retirement and brokerage accounts you used to own.
(beat)
Al, the mortgage on your Montana property has been foreclosed,
(to Mark)
as have your properties in Lausanne, Mark.
(to John)
The property in La Jolla, John. And just to add some incentives, you all have liens placed on them by the IRS.

JOHN
Bullshit.

STAN
You know the trusts that have been set up in the names of your grandchildren, wives, and former employees? They have all been likened

and held. Do you have a cell phone? Check it
out.

                                    CUT TO:

INT. WATSON HOME, KITCHEN, ARLINGTON,
VIRGINIA - DAY

Rodney looks through the drawers and then
checks the front of the refrigerator, looking for information. His search is quick and
precise.

INT. WATSON HOME, MASTER BEDROOM, ARLINGTON,
VIRGINIA - DAY

Wilbur looks through papers and a date book
on the desk. By the look on his face, he has
found something. He holds a flight schedule. He
hears a police SIREN. We see him running down
the stairs to the living room.

INT. WATSON HOME, LIVING ROOM, ARLINGTON,
VIRGINIA - DAY

Wilbur enters with a flight schedule in his
hand as Rodney enters from the kitchen.

WILBUR
They may be headed for Jamaica. We better
check connecting flights and see.

                                    CUT TO:

EXT. BURNING TREE GOLF CLUB, TERRACE - DAY

Stan slams the men who believed they had him
by the short hairs.

AL
Assuming you were able to do all of this,
Stan, it will only be a matter of time until
we straighten all this out.

STAN
It gets worse. Starting next week, depend-
ing on your performance, one by one, the same
thing will happen to all of your Board members and relatives. Guess who is on top of the
list? The vice president, Dave Abrams. I want
his resignation on my desk as soon as these
bills are on my desk for signature.

John and Mark make calls, while Al sits quietly staring at Stan.

                                    CUT TO:

INT. WATSON HOME, LIVING ROOM, ARLINGTON,
VIRGINIA - DAY

POLICE OFFICER LIGHTFOOT (35, Caucasian) and
OFFICER KINNEY (30, Hispanic) appear in the
doorway with weapons raised.

OFFICER KINNEY
(To Wilbur and Rodney)
Raise your hands slowly.

WILBUR
Officers, we are Secret Service agents on an
errand for the president.

OFFICER LIGHTFOOT
What errand might that be?

RODNEY

May we show you some identification?

OFFICER KINNEY
Reach for it slowly with your left hand, and
place it on the table.

Wilbur reaches inside his coat and presents ID.
As everyone relaxes a bit, Wilbur extends the
ID to Kinney, with the other hand brings a gun
from behind him, and shoots Officer Lightfoot
in the shoulder.

Officer Kinney fires directly at Rodney, killing
him. Wilbur fires again, wounding Kinney, and
they roll on the floor. Lightfoot manages to
kick the gun out of Wilbur's hand, and Wilbur
expertly wriggles out of Kinney's grasp and
disappears through the front door.

EXT. WATSON HOME, ARLINGTON, VIRGINIA - DAY

Rubber smokes from the government vehicle
screeching out of the Watson driveway into the
quiet street.

                                        CUT TO:

EXT. BURNING TREE GOLF CLUB, TERRACE - DAY

Stan, Mark, Al, and John continue their heated
conversation.

STAN
Along with the bills, I also want cashier's
checks on my desk by tomorrow at 8:00 am for
your losses today. John, $120,000, Mark,
$80,000 and you, Al, $60,000. You all will
retire from active corporate life and give me

each forty hours a week of volunteer time as mentors for my youth program, five years each.

AL
I have difficulty believing you have the infra-structure to execute all of this.

STAN
Try me. If the checks aren't on my desk tomor-row and the bills passed a week from today at noon, I will immediately put into action the chaos I have described. I understand that you will have to assess the current damage and see if you think I have the capacity to back it up.

AL
Are you sure you want to put the rest of your family in jeopardy like this?

STAN
Even if you take me and my family, there are too many people involved and committed to this for you and generations of your families to ever recover.
(Beat)
John, you ever been on welfare? Mark, have you ever stood in line for food stamps?

MARK
No, and neither have you. I worked three jobs to get through school. I worked hard for every dime I have.

STAN
Isn't it strange how some people distance themselves from the very people who made it possible for them to advance? Have you ever

noticed that some people who come up through the ranks take on the same inhumane way of treating people below them, the same crummy way they were treated? I am making it possible for you to change that.
Are you sure you want to put the rest of your family in jeopardy like this?
Don't take it personal, boys. It's just business.
(holds up Codex book)

                                        CUT TO:

INT. MARIETTA'S HOUSE, BEDROOM, JAMAICA - DAY

The rising sun shines on Bertie's face. Marietta rushes in to wake her and Alice.

MARIETTA
Wake up, Bertie, Alice. I just spoke with Stan. They know you're
here. We have to hide you somewhere else. Hurry, get dressed.

Bertie and Alice dress and throw clothes in their suitcases.

MARIETTA (CONT'D)
Hurry! Go out the back. There you will find a shed. There is a trap door, which leads to a tunnel. It will take you to the street. Somebody will be waiting for you to take you to the airport.

BERTIE
Thank you, Marietta. Be safe.

They hug, and Bertie and Alice run out the door.

INT. MARIETTA'S HOUSE, LIVING ROOM, JAMAICA - DAY

Within minutes, Wilbur kicks in the front door and grabs Marietta by the throat, her feet slightly lifted from floor.

WILBUR
I know they've been here. I'll burn this shack to the ground with you in it, old woman.

MARIETTA
(choking)
Your name Wilbur?

WILBUR
Yeah, who wants to know?

MARIETTA
(phone in hand)
A call for you.

Marietta slowly hands him the phone.

WILBUR
(on phone)
Yes, sir, will do. Abort it is.

He releases her. She coughs and rubs her throat.

WILBUR (CONT'D)
Sorry for the inconvenience. Have a nice day.

Wilbur runs out of the house.

MARIETTA
Have a nice day?

                              CUT TO:

INT. WHITE HOUSE, OVAL OFFICE, WASHINGTON DC
- DAY

Stan sits at his desk typing on the computer.

STAN (V.O.)
(types on computer)
Plan B, everyone. Initiate Humpty Dumpty on
the Board of Directors at Chevron, AT&T, and
Ford.

                              CUT TO:

INT. SWISS PRISON, SMALL ROOM, GENEVA - DAY

Alex sits in an isolated room with a PRISON
GUARD standing at the door with his back to
him, as he sends a message on a small laptop
computer.

ALEX (V.O.)
(types on computer)
Hershell, are you there? I have the bank
and stock account numbers. Are you ready to
receive?

                              CUT TO:

INT. HOUSE, BEDROOM, OAKLAND, CALIFORNIA
- DAY

Hershell sits at a computer communicating with

Alex. We see Alex's message on his computer screen. He types, "READY."

HERSHELL
Here they come.

Names, account numbers, and bank information are downloaded. Then Hershell types, "Anita, Nisha, and Mc Crae, are you ready?" He receives their message on the screen: "Ready."

CUT TO:

INT. WHITE HOUSE, OVAL OFFICE, WASHINGTON DC - DAY

Stan receives a message on his computer screen, "Good luck. I'm signing off. Keep me posted, Alex." Stan turns off the computer when Elsie enters with important papers.

ELSIE
Mr. President, these checks arrived by messenger, sir.

STAN
Golf winnings, Elsie.

ELSIE
You must have a very low handicap, sir.

STAN
I have absolutely none whatsoever.

CUT TO:

EXT. SWISS PRISON, GENEVA - NIGHT

REPORTERS swarm around the exit where SPECTATORS holding the American flag cheer and wave as Alex Rutherford, Peter Straus, Wilson Powers, Franklin Steadman, Floyd Davidson, Edna Addington, Cameron Shaherazad, Louis Solomon, and Rishad Ali exit. NEWS REPORTER #3 (African American man) says –

NEWS REPORTER #3
(To Alex)
Alex Rutherford, the Humpty Dumpties have been exonerated and you are now all heroes. How does it feel being responsible for bringing down the man who bombed the plane, killing the president's grandson?

CUT TO:

INT. TELECOMMUNICATIONS BUILDING, SATELLITE OFFICE – DAY

The FBI handcuffs BOMBER, a.k.a. satellite specialist, and takes him out as his CO-WORKERS watch.

Alex (V.O.)
The satellite specialist who was spying for major corporations was also the bomber.

BACK TO:

EXT. SWISS PRISON, GENEVA – NIGHT

News Reporter #3 interviews Alex.

ALEX
(to reporter)
Truth has set us free and has chained our

adversary. The taste of freedom is sweet. Thank you.

The Egghead Group walks into the crowd of cheering spectators.

                                    CUT TO:

INT. WHITE HOUSE, WATSON RESIDENCE, LIVING ROOM - NIGHT

Bertie and Alice enter with suitcases and set them down in the foyer. Stan glides in and embraces Bertie and Alice.

STAN
Thank God, my girls are safe.
(To Bertie)
My sweet love, how I adore you.

He takes her by the hands and dances with her, spins her, and then a dip.

STAN (CONT'D)
I have something to tell you. Sit, my dear.
(Bertie sits)
I'll be right back.

He goes back to the foyer where Alice is stand-ing and touches her face.

STAN (CONT'D)
My baby. You are my treasure. I am so sorry, honey, about Mattie. She will never be forgotten.

ALICE
(eyes well up)

Dad …

STAN
No … you mean so much to me. Honey, you will
have another child. Who knows, maybe twins.
Someone is here to see you. Forgive him, baby.
Life is too short to have differences stand
between you.

They hug, and Stan kisses her on the cheek,
then dances her to the bedroom door where she
sees her HUSBAND (35, African American, handsome man), from whom she has been separated.
Alice enters the bedroom. They cry, embrace,
and kiss. Stan closes the door.

Stan enters the living room and sits in a
chair in front of Bertie. He takes her hand.

STAN (CONT'D)
I found something.

BERTIE
What?

STAN
When I was a boy, we were poor. I wanted to
help my parents, so I climbed a mango tree that
was in our backyard and threw down the mangos
so I could sell them. Then I lost my balance
and fell through the outhouse into sewage. I
was stuck there up to my neck. I screamed out
to my father. He came outside, saw me, and
punished me by leaving me there all day. That
pit of sewage was a place of horror, and in
the darkness, I cried. From that time on, when
I was lonely or hurt, I locked myself in the
closet, punishing myself as my father did.

Then I decided to have a heart of stone so no one could hurt me. Remember me telling you about the boy, Stone Paxton?

Bertie nods.

DISSOLVE TO:

EXT. GROCERY STORE, OAKLAND, CALIFORNIA - DAY (FLASHBACK)

Outside a small grocery store, Stone Paxton has just made a transaction with a user when a limousine pulls up. Stone walks up to the vehicle. The window is lowered, revealing -

INT. LIMOUSINE, OAKLAND, CALIFORNIA - DAY (FLASHBACK)

Stan sits in limo when the boy, Stone, approaches him.

STAN (V.O.)
Well, that was me. I wasn't selling drugs, I just had a bad attitude and felt unloved. And then Stone said -

STONE
You see, Mr. President, I can't read.

STAN (V.O.)
I could read, I just couldn't read into the hearts of those around me. When he touched my face and said -

STAN
Stone, I need your help to change all of this, so that people are

safe in their beds at night, not afraid of
being shot by a stray bullet.
(lifts Stone's head)
Will you help me?

                                   BACK TO:

INT. WHITE HOUSE, WATSON RESIDENCE, LIVING
ROOM - NIGHT

Bertie listens to the heart of her man, her
king.

STAN
I knew I was a part of him, that he had love
for me. He cared in a way no one ever has, and
in my mind, he would be my father, a father
of hope. So I held him near to my heart, and
I stopped locking myself in a closet, crying,
feeling forgotten, and I promised that I would
never forget the "Forgotten People."

                                   DISSOLVE TO:

INT. EAST MIDDLE SCHOOL, AUDITORIUM, OAKLAND,
CALIFORNIA - DAY (FLASHBACK)

Stan walks out on stage. Stone turns and sticks
his tongue out at his friends and claps quick
and hard. The teachers and children stand
cheering.

STAN (V.O.)
And that day when the first black president
made a speech at my
school, I knew that would be me. From that
moment on, I fought for love.

CUT TO:

INT. WHITE HOUSE, WATSON RESIDENCE, LIVING
ROOM – NIGHT

Bertie is touched by Stan's story.

STAN
I knew I would find it, so I could give it to
the world. My suffering became my stone, the
one I would stand upon, and build from there.
When the boy, Stone Paxton, said, "I was sorry
to hear 'bout your granddaughter," it was as
if I knew my own destiny, but could not stop
what would happen.

Alice and her husband stand in the doorway as
tears come down. They enter, and then sat.

BERTIE
So the president really wasn't there.

DISSOLVE TO:

EXT. GROCERY STORE, OAKLAND, CALIFORNIA – DAY
(FLASHBACK)

A homeless man (45, Caucasian) and a few children hang out on the corner as usual. PULL
BACK TO REVEAL Stone Paxton holding a Diet
Pepsi talking to himself at curbside, using
hand gestures.

STAN (V.O.)
Right. Just a boy who found hope.

HOMELESS MAN
Who is he talking to?

STAN (V.O.)
After he touched my heart, I was free from the
chains of despair and poverty. He enriched
me, giving me hope to aspire, and I did. Do
you understand? What I aspired to be became
my hope; it came to life, the president. Then
Stone Paxton disappeared like a cloud in the
wind.

Stone Paxton disappears before the homeless
man's eyes. Shocked, he drops his alcohol bottle in a paper bag.

STAN (V.O. CONT'D)
Then as a man, I started having dreams, dreams
of heroes, those who have touched the world
with greatness.

                                    DISSOLVE TO:

EXT. CARIBBEAN BEACH, JAMAICA - NIGHT
(FLASHBACK)

Stan walks along the beach with his father
holding the Holy Bible. They walk toward the
same bonfire. Stan's father stops, smiles, then
fades away.

STAN (V.O.)
I dreamed of my father the way I wanted him to
be a man of God, a man of strength and hope.

Then Stan looks toward a circle of people:
Abe Lincoln sits with Martin Luther King Jr.,
Thomas Jefferson, Frederick Douglass, Crazy
Horse, Harriet Tubman, W. E. B. Dubois, Sitting
Bull, César Chavez, and Duke Ellington.

STAN (V.O. CONT'D)
And in my despair, a place of darkness, I
would dream, and my dreams empowered me.

CUT TO:

INT. WHITE HOUSE, WATSON RESIDENCE, LIVING
ROOM - NIGHT

Stan talks with his family.

STAN
Bertie, I found the missing piece. I am the
father of many, and the people are my children. None will be forgotten.

BERTIE
Stan …

ALICE
Dad, what an incredible story.

Stan hands Bertie a sealed envelope.

BERTIE
What's this?
(Opens envelope)
A paternity test?

STAN
I was never unfaithful to you. Not even for a
moment. In our troubled time, I met a young
pregnant woman who wanted to die. She did not
want to carry the shame alone, so I vowed she
could say that I was Thomas's father.

ALICE

Why didn't you tell the people?

STAN
Should I crucify him that I may be free and
he carry the shame? No, therefore, I will die
with the truth so he is spared. He was forgotten by his father, but not by me.

BERTIE
I'm speechless.

STAN
I stand against the bullet of defeat. I am no
longer a boy with a stone heart but a man full
of love. I stand for the poor and the hungry.
I will be a shield against injustice. I do not
stand for the system. It was the system that
oppressed the people. Therefore, in my suffering, I "**Cry Freedom**" and I took my cries to
the people of the world.

Everyone gets up and hugs Stan.

ALICE
Wow, Dad. I never knew. Isn't tomorrow night
the memorial for the forgotten people?

STAN
Yes, but maybe no one will show up. It may
just be us, but however it will be, the stars
will shine.

INT. WHITE HOUSE, WATSON RESIDENCE, OFFICE
- NIGHT

It's pitch black. Stan, who sits at his desk,
turns on the lights. He slowly looks up when
he hears a VOICE.

MALE NARRATOR (V.O.)
Stan, if you do not expose the leaders of the
United States and the heads of countries, you
stand with them. You will allow the chains of
oppression to remain, use your ace card and
play the hand you were dealt. You were chosen
to save the people. Truth is the key. Free
them.

CUT TO:

INT. WHITE HOUSE, EAST ROOM, WASHINGTON DC
- DAY

Stan holds a press conference. We see the name
tags of the newly appointed members to the
White House. REPORTERS flash cameras.

Secretary of State Alex Rutherford, Secretary
of Human Resources Edna Addington, Secretary
of Urban Affairs Wilson Powers, Secretary
of Science and Technology Peter Straus, and
Secretary of Education Floyd Davidson.

STAN
The federal government of the United States
and foreign governments, banks, and some
Fortune 500 companies were actively involved
in, and profited from, gold and slave trading.
The richest corporations in the US, which is
an international corporation today, made billions of dollars long ago in the trading of
gold and slaves.
(Holds up Codex)
Proof of this information has already been given
to the U.S. and the international press.

NEWS REPORTER (35, African American woman) stands.

NEWS REPORTER #4
Mr. President, is it true that Vice President David Abrams, corporate heads Al Smith, Mark Turner, and John Wentworth were the masterminds of your grandson's, Mattie's, and Gene Radamier's murders?

CUT TO:

INT. POLICE STATION, BOOKING ROOM, WASHINGTON DC - DAY

David Abrams, Al Smith, Mark Turner, and John Wentworth are handcuffed, numbered, and photographed.

CUT TO:

EXT. MONUMENT/FORGOTTEN PEOPLE, WASHINGTON DC - NIGHT

Near the Lincoln Memorial, flags encircle a beautiful monument. Overhead view of the circular open structure, which is four walls with equal entrances that divide them. Each wall has countless pictures of people on it. In the center are statues of an ethnic diversity of people including children gathered together. There are no people in sight until Stan speaks.

SLOW PAN over title on the wall, "THE FORGOTTEN PEOPLE," then over the pictures on the wall, then the title below the pictures, "You will never be forgotten. You are stars in the night."

Stan, Bertie, their grandchildren, Alice and her husband, stand on stage with Secret Service all around.

Unknown to Stan, PEOPLE are grouped by race outside the monument. As he speaks, they enter and come together as one, hugging, kissing, and smiling at each other. Thousands gather.

STAN
We shall overcome prejudices, racial conflict, division, and hate with love, and violence with peace. We shall overcome. We shall overcome poverty with generosity, a coldness of heart with warmth, hunger with sharing. We will be blameless against each other because we stand as one. We shall overcome. We thank Abe Lincoln, Martin Luther King Jr., Nelson Mandela, Malcolm X, Thurgood Marshall, Crazy Horse, Harriet Tubman, W. E. B. Dubois, Frederick Douglass, César Chavez, and countless more. They laid the stones to the crossing of the bridge to freedom.

We see Stan's estranged daughter, his son-in-law, Raymond, Buck and Melvin, the Native American family, the old woman, Marietta, Ruth Festoonie and child, the taxi driver, George, the White House butler/driver, Nisha, Anita, Mc Crae, Hershell, Anthony, and Alex, Franklin, Edna, Wilson, Cameron, Louis, Peter, Floyd, and Rishad.

STAN (CONT'D)
And so, my fellow Americans, at this, my third

State of the Union, I come before you with the sense that we are all on a new path. I want to congratulate all of you and thank you for beginning the journey with me, to return this wonderful country to a place where more of us can enjoy it. Because we love God, America, and ourselves, may our actions always be motivated by love, and may God's grace always shine on thee. God bless America.

Then we see the boy, Stone Paxton, wave at Stan. Stan winks and smiles, then Stone disappear. Fireworks go off. Then Stan shouts, "Yes we can," with arms toward the sky, then the people join in. It's truly a historic moment.

STAN (CONT'D)
Yes we can! Yes we can! Yes we can! Yes we can! Yes we can! Yes we can! Yes we can!

PEOPLE
Yes we can! Yes we can! Yes we can! Yes we can! Yes we can! Yes we can!

The people ROAR as Stan steps down, shaking hands, as he and his family exit. Then MUSIC, "The Humpty Dumpty," plays and Stan, his family, and the people the audience recognizes follow him out dancing. Then all the people dance.

                                        CUT TO:

INT. LIMOUSINE, WASHINGTON DC - NIGHT

Stan and Bertie cuddle in the back. MUSIC plays in the limo: the "Beige Movement" from Duke Ellington's *Black, Brown, and Beige.*

STAN
All I ever wanted is sitting right next to me.
I love you, Bertie.
(They kiss)
I'm the president. We can do anything we
want.

BERTIE
Anything?

STAN
Within reason. I'm an old guy, you know.

BERTIE
Come here, you old guy. My hero.

EXT. LIMOUSINE, WASHINGTON DC - NIGHT

Long SHOT on the limo, taking in Capitol Hill,
then WIDER on Washington lit up at night, with
the new memorial prominent.

                              FADE OUT.

As CREDITS roll, the narrator speaks.

NARRATOR (V.O.)
Recognizing the human desire and spirit to
exercise self-determination, and to pursue
life, freedom, and happiness. Because of historical facts and events, let us put into context and perspective that we hold these truths
to be self-evident and relevant, that "all
men" were created equal. But because of certain inherent characteristics, they were not
allowed the same opportunity to pursue their
dreams and fulfill their destinies to exploit

their fullest potential in achieving all that they were ordained and destined to have for themselves and their offspring. They had the right to freedom then, you have the right to freedom now and in the future.
(Beat)
You have the right to collect for your ancestors everything that's owed to them, and to use and invest these assets for your progeny into perpetuity, and to pass on your history, culture, traditions, knowledge, wealth, and family spirit. This is a fundamental right all people possess. To this end, we have established a fund of five trillion dollars in gold, in a numbered Swiss account, code name "The Twenty-First Century Project - Code: 12 / 15 / 22 / 5." These funds are for education, the uplifting and elevation of your massive underclass, and to ensure that all the nations in the "New World Order" survive through the twenty-first century. The Codex is a book of alchemy containing the formula for turning baser metals into gold. "Yes We Can" and "Yes We Did."

To: *The Keeper of the Flame,*
President Stanley Watson

From: Martin Luther King Jr.

I HAD A DREAM!

Life, liberty, and the pursuit of happiness are what that dream was. Persistence, dedication, and audacity are the sparks that ignite the flame that burns across the hearts and souls of man and transforms dreams into reality. The promise of America will not be extinguish from the earth because of any one person or persons; men come and go, but America and the world will live on forever.

As long as God continues to shine his light on America and we continue to reaffirm, sustain, and advance the promise of America, our future looks promising.

This great country was founded on principles that time and space, man or beast, cannot deter or eliminate. Our path has been laid out from the founding of the world. Our job is to fulfill our destiny. You have been chosen to advance and sustain our foundation of hope and to create a sustainable future at this time in our county's history.

The eagle is sick, its feathers are falling off, its vision is clouded, and it's being strangled because we have allowed the forces of evil to infect our nation's mind, body, and soul. This is why you are called at this time.

Your presidency is a patriotic and necessary

endeavor. You will be one of the cornerstones for a new America—vital to the rebuilding of America's foundation and character. All great societies need men like you.

You have many gifts; your spirit and civic-mindedness will not be denied a place in history. "Never give up—never, never, never give up." Your persistence and dedication to America's promise is your calling.

Thank you for your faith in America and the world. May God grant you wisdom, strength, and a clear vision to see this masterpiece of statesmanship to its completion.

America has been the inspiration and foundation of my life. I did all that I could to advance and sustain this foundation. We are all bound by duty and honor to leave a legacy for future generations of Americans and to inspire the world to reach that shinning city on the hill, where the air is clear and clean, so that the great eagle will become healthy again, to fly high and proud, so that liberty and freedom will have a chance to survive. It is the least we can do as Americans and citizens of the world.

Mr. President, you are a great American. Long life and good health to you and your family. May the blessing of liberty forever inflame your love and passion. Cry freedom! So, after all these years of restlessness, the dream is now a reality. Your ancestors and I can finally get some rest.

May you bless and change America and the world.

MLK

LIGHTS. CAMERA. ACTION!

I have lived and worked in Hollywood since 1992. I went to film school at LA City College and worked for Paramount Studio and several independent film and production companies. I have respect for the creative professionals that run and control Hollywood. However, in Hollywood, projects are chosen and produced through a fiery and complex series of detailed reasons that only the inside circle controls. In all fairness, there are thousands of scripts written every year and only a few get produced; that's why there is such a need for independent film companies like Cry Freedom Pictures.

The limitations on what gets made and when are the reasons why we have decided to go below, above, and around the wall of Hollywood. My appeal to you, the public, is that if you would love to be part of the foundation of this project, together we *can* produce this movie. This will be the first publicly produced and financed movie brought to life by the citizens of the globe. Hollywood can help if they are moved by the financial or historical content of this project … only time will tell if they choose to do so.

At this time in history, we are the stars, the movers and shakers: you, me, and us. Your donations at this grassroots level will make this movie a reality. All it takes is pennies and volumes of love and support, and we can create the foundation for a successful project. Tell your family, friends, and everyone you can to invest all of your pennies, because it's the foundation of dollars … *let's change the system!*

To my fellow writers: Creative brothers and sisters, you have spent years of your lives, invested your money, sacrificed time with your family and friends, and spent sleepless nights locked away in your private world working on your passion, only to have it rejected or only to be given a small, inadequate amount of compensation, without the respect deserved or access to the production process. You watch your creation be changed or alerted, and sometimes completely reconstructed, with credit given to the new owners as authors. We have accepted this for too long … *let's change the system!*

We all have the freedom to choose the path we will walk in our lives and careers. So, my fellow writers, your Eppieologist recommends that you write, publish, produce, and direct your own projects. Without our creative energy and passion, there will be no movies. Remember, it all starts with an idea.

It's the public who has made and keeps Hollywood sustainable and profitable. You have started the campaign for freedom today by purchasing *The President /The Eppieologist*. Elect Stanley Watson for president, and help finance/produce *The President* the movie with me.

In closing, "Never give up—never, never, never."
This is a movie, a Hollywood fantasy, and a dream.

Dreams are the foundation of reality, so let us all *wake up*!

America's first black president? You must be kidding. It's impossible! Not in my or your lifetime. Hell has frozen over!

Let's "change the world, and make it a better place."

Yes We Should, Yes We Can, & Yes We Did …
SEE YOU AT THE MOVIES!

LOVE & HONOR

*

Love, Strength and Honor from me and the recipients of you generous contributions to the Freedom Foundation Inc. because of your purchase of "THE PRSIDENT' / "THE EPPIEOLOGIST."

This is the beginning of a historical and entertaining journey into the world of Movies and Reality. If you would love to see this project on the big screen at your local movie theater and be a share holder in CRY FREEDOM PICTURES and a supporter and member of CRY FREEDOM FOUNDATION INC. do it for yourself and to leave a legacy for your family, friends and the world; create your gift of love that will live on into perpetuity.

"THE PRESIDENT" / "THE EPPIEOLOGIST"

*Staring:
President?

First Lady?

*Director:
Eppie Elkahan

*Producers:
Eppie Elkahan / The World

Cry Freedom Pictures / Island Production are holding a casting call for an important role in a MAJOR MOTION PICTURE; it's about the first black President of the United States.

The call is for the President and First Lady.

This is not a comedy, but a serious political drama, that has all of the elements that produces Academy Award Winners.

We are not looking for established Hollywood actors but actors with a passion and talent to add gravitas to the script "THE PRESIDENT" / "THE EPPIEOLOGIST."

If you would love to run for President of the United States this is your history making moment.

Your campaign begins today!

Your Love, Energy and Passion will sustain the path and support the journey to documenting this revolutionary and historical presidency.

Epaphroditus "Eppie" Elkahan

"The last living decedent of the Goddess of LOVE Aphrodite."

Live, Love and Die with passion!

Cry Freedom Pictures
P.O. Box 574, Pacific Grove, CA 93950
Tel. (917) 456.2194

Web Site: www.cryfreedompictures.com
E-Mail: cryfreedompictures@yahoo.com

"CRY FREEDOM FOUNDATION"

*

World Vision

MISSION STATEMENT

THE GIFT OF LOVE * THE FRUIT OF LIFE

Cry Freedom Foundation Inc. is a Non Profit 501(c) 3 tax exempt organization which mission is the liberation of any human from all things that prevent them or diminishes their achievements of life by providing food, clothing, shelter, health services, social, academic and educational support to family's and individuals.

These services will Inspire, Motivate, Encourage and Support them as they work towards a sustainable life; we will help them to achieve their ultimate potential.

We will collaborate with citizens of the world who give of themselves Mind, Body, Soul and Love. Our time and love are the fruit of life.

As we continue this historical journey of change around the world it's not enough just to give financial support, we must get involved in our communities. We must give our love, time and passion to elevate and improve the human condition.

"Helping people to break free from whatever
enslaves them is our goal."

The liberation of any human from all things
that prevent them or diminishes their achievements of Life, Liberty and Happiness is the
ultimate expression of the un-conditional gift
of Love that any human can give or transfer to
another.

Today there are lots of issues that are vying
for our time and attention in this ever chang-
ing world. As citizens of this world we know
our history and some of the issues we have
struggle with and have found solution for.
In the past whenever we have faced challenges
that threaten our future as a planet, we have
always risen to the occasion.

Our ability to change or create is what makes
us unique, but there are some things we must
never change. As we look through history every
civilization started its decline when the basic
foundation of its existence that supports
the family tree was allowed to deteriorate.
Eventually the fabric of its existence died
and the branches were cut off and destroyed.
As a planet made up of families that have sacrificed and contributed to the making of this
world, our diversity is one of the pillars of
our strength and this has contributed to making us strong and resplendent.

Some fellow humans think we have lost the ability to inspire and motivate, only you can be
the judge of this kind of thinking, I refuse
to believe that. This leads me to conclude
that there are many wide and varied opinions

on this subject, which is not necessarily bad. Self analysis is to be encouraged, as a fellow citizen and a father of five children I have raise my children to respect the planet, people and to be productive citizens as they advance the human condition.

But I find myself dismayed by the very system that encourages us to be loving, caring, sensitive and compassionate to one another, will at the same time leave its most valuable assets, vulnerable to hostile and predatory elements that inhabit our world today. A great humanitarian once said: "The true test of any nation's determination and ability to shape and control it's future depends on it's skills at encouraging and inspiring the citizens of it's society to achieve the highest yield and rewards from the seeds planted in prior generations."

The disintegration of the world's family troubles me greatly. It doesn't matter who you are or where you live. Our lives now and in the future are extricable built and sustained on the foundation of our family's. We all have a tremendous responsibility to show the "Gift of Love" that was given to us and to be able to assist those in need of encouragement and human support.

I give my respect, strength and honor to all fellow humans that support or provide any assistance to citizens of the world; it does not matter how big or small your contribution is. If you assist people you are a humanitarian. We are all gifts of love, we must make the way as well prepared as possible to ensure that every human be given the opportunity to pursue life, liberty and to achieve happiness as they reach their full potential in a sustainable way. By doing this we shall all benefit and our planet will derive untold blessing from our efforts.

For these reasons and others I founded Cry Freedom Foundation that seeks to further the cause of human development and to ensure future generations all the best we can leave them to guarantee the worlds future. Only by doing this we will keep the planet sustainable and an inspiration for us all. In the real world money is one of the tools needed to promote and advance any cause especially one as important as this.

So we are asking for your generous donations and contributions to "CRY FREEDOM FOUNDATION INC" * "THE INSTITUTE FOR THE STUDIES, ADVANCEMENT AND PRESAVATION OF ALL HUMANS." These funds will be used to provide comprehensive research and studies into how we as citizens of the world can insure that all people get all the basic spiritual, humanitarian, health, nutritional, academic, medical, scientific, technological, social, and psychological support. Like the Mission Statement proclaims Freedom of our Mind, Body and Soul, from whatever enslave us as humans, should be the primary focus of all countries of this planet. This planet has all the elements and resources, air, land and sea to support and sustain every human that exist in this circular place we call home.

If you subscribe to these Eppieological ideas, ideals, thoughts, concepts and strategies will you please support this humanitarian gift of love. If you cannot provide financial support, will you consider becoming a volunteer member and contribute your time and expertise to this cause.

We believe your attention to this most critical human endeavor will ensure a bright, prosperous and sustainable world; if you would write or call and offer your suggestions on how you think we can take the human race off the endangered species list and to preserve it into universal infinity. We would love to hear from you today. We value you thoughts, encouragement and love.

Religion and Politics should be tools we use to support and advance all humans.

The love of money is the root of all evil.

The love of humans is the root of all good.

Live, Love and Die with passion!

Donations and Contribution are tax deductible and allow by law and for any question or information please go to:
www.cryfreedomfoundation.com

THE GIFT OF LOVE
*
THE FRUIT OF LIFE

THE INSTANT WE ENTER THIS WORLD,
WE GIVE AND WE TAKE OF LOVE.

THIS IS THE MOMENT WE COME TO LIFE,
WE SHARE OF LOVE AND GIVE TO LIFE.

SO IF WE ARE THE FRUITS OF LOVE,
WE SHOULD MAKE LOVE THE GIFT OF LIFE.

LET US SHARE THIS MOST PRECIOUS GIFT
WITH THOSE WHO ARE IN NEED OF LOVE,
SO THAT THEIR LIVES MAY TAKE ROOT AND GROW.

AS CUSTODIANS OF THIS MOST PRECIOUS GIFT,
LET'S REPLENISH WHAT WE TAKE FROM LOVE
SO THAT OTHERS MAY HAVE THE FULL WELL OF LOVE
TO DRAW FROM TO ENRICH THEIR LIVES.

AS WE WATER THE GARDEN OF LOVE,
WE MAKE SWEET ALL WHO WE MEET IN LIFE.

WE HELP THEM TO MATURE AND PROGRESS
AND REACH THEIR FULL POTENTIAL.
AND BY DOING THIS MOST UNSELFISH ACT,
WE REPLANT THE SEED THAT STARTED US.

SO THAT ANOTHER LIFE MAY EXPERIENCE
THE GIFT OF LOVE, THE FRUIT OF LIFE.

The Eppieologist